QUICK & EASY, PROVEN RECIPES

Barbecue

Publisher's Note: Raw or semi-cooked eggs should not be consumed by babies, toddlers,
pregnant or breastfeeding women, the elderly or those suffering from a chronic illness.

Publisher & Creative Director: Nick Wells
Project Editor: Catherine Taylor
Art Director: Mike Spender
Layout Design: Federica Ciaravella
Digital Design & Production: Chris Herbert

Special thanks to Gina Steer, Steven Morris, Sally Davis, Kelly Auricchio and Frances Bodiam.

FLAME TREE PUBLISHING
6 Melbray Mews, Fulham,
London SW6 3NS
United Kingdom
flametreepublishing.com

18 20 22 21 19
1 3 5 7 9 10 8 6 4 2

ISBN: 978-1-78664-786-3

Printed in China

QUICK & EASY, PROVEN RECIPES

Barbecue

General Editor: Gina Steer

FLAME TREE
PUBLISHING

Contents

Essentials

Before we get into the recipes, brush up on the basics. Learn about the different types of barbecue available and the best tools for flipping those burgers, along with tips for preparing and cooking your food. We also provide some delicious recipes for butters, coatings and marinades, which will really give your food added zing. Last but not least, refresh your memory on fundamental hygiene rules and the key elements of nutrition.

Barbecues

Barbecuing is the perfect way to entertain both family and friends. However, sometimes even the most confident person can be put off – who wants to cook in front of an audience and get it wrong? As a result, many barbecues sit on a patio or terrace neglected and forlorn, hardly used except for the occasional sausage. Well read on – this book will change all that. Read this introduction first so you are completely familiar with the basics of barbecuing and have a few trial runs before embarking on a full-scale party.

Choosing Your Barbecue

Before buying, consider which barbecue is right for you. First consider the size – how many will you be cooking for? And how often will you use it? It's not worth spending masses if you are only going to use it occasionally. Where will you use it and store it? Which type of fuel do you favour? And of course, what will you cook? All these points must be considered.

Types of Barbecue

There are six main types of barbecues in varying sizes and prices, all with their pros and cons.

- Charcoal Barbecue – The traditional choice, there are many charcoal (or wood burning) barbecues to choose from, ranging in price and sophistication. The very simplest consists of a tray on legs with an adjustable grill rack. They can be free-standing or simply placed on a sturdy surface such as a specially built wide wall. The fuel is placed in the tray and lit at least 20–30 minutes before using, or longer. This allows the smoke to disperse and the coals to become hot. The food is placed on the grill rack for cooking.

For more sophisticated barbecues, look for adjustable air vents which help to control the flow of air and thus the temperature. Or check out barbecues which boast a rotisserie and hood, making them ideal for indirect grilling, cooking whole chickens or larger fish.

∾ **Kettle Barbecues** – Also free-standing, the domed lid makes kettle barbecues ideal for both grilling and roasting and perfect for cooking whole fish – much in the same way as an oven. Two methods of heating are available, either charcoal or gas-fuelled.

∾ **Built-in Barbecues** – These barbecues are normally permanent fixtures and are often placed in the garden where there is plenty of room for seating. A chimney can be used to take the smoke away from the immediate area.

∾ **Gas Barbecues** – Fuelled normally by bottled butane and propane gas, these consist of a trolley with a thermometer located inside the hood and the gas bottle stored in the cupboard underneath. The grill rack is inset into the trolley with work areas on at least one side but often on both. Often a small burner is on one of the sides for the preparation of sauces. Stir-fries can be cooked on this.

Essentials

The heat is measured in BTU (British Thermal Units). Look for two elements rather than one as two give a more even distribution of heat; these are made either from stainless steel or iron (remember that iron tends to rust), while lava rock or ceramic stones help prevent the gas jets from becoming blocked with meat juices or fat. The temperature is very easy to control but do ensure that the knobs are sturdy.

- Electric Barbecues – These operate in a very similar manner to the oven in your kitchen. They are the easiest to use and control due to their thermostatic controls, which almost guarantee perfect results every time.

- Disposable Barbecues – These can only be used once and are normally quite small. They consist of a lightweight foil tray filled with charcoal (treated for easy ignition). Check whether you are allowed to use them in your chosen area, as many picnic areas forbid their use. Take care in their disposal.

Types of Fuel

- Wood – Hard wood, rather than soft, is best for burning on the barbecue. The smell and taste of foods cooked in wood smoke is wonderful – look for wood that gives off a particular perfume when burning, such as pine. Hickory wood is popular for its flavour. Wood is not that easy to light but burns quickly, so the barbecue quickly becomes cold unless the cooking process is interrupted with more wood being added. Time must be taken for the heat to return.

- Lumpwood charcoal – This is made from wood that has been fired in a kiln. It is extremely easy to light. As it has already reached the charcoal stage there is less waiting than with hard wood. Look for larger pieces rather than the small.

- Briquettes – These are crushed charcoal, with starch added as a binder, and are an excellent heat source. The best are made from crushed coconut shells as they hold the heat for longer. Some may be 'self lighting' – so-called because paraffin or petroleum has usually been added to aid ignition.

Barbecue Tools

Once you have selected which barbecue is for you, it is time to consider the tools you will require.

- ༀ Tongs – A sturdy pair of tongs is essential – look for ones that have heat-resistant handles and grippers that will not damage the cooked foods. A second pair is good for turning the coals over or helping with the food.

- ༀ Long-Handled Fork – A long-handled fork is ideal for turning steaks, chops, sausages and all firmer foods. It is also good for checking if the food is cooked.

- ༀ Long-Handled Fish Slice – As the name suggests, this is perfect for turning whole fish over. Two is even better.

- ༀ Hinged baskets – These are perfect for cooking whole fish, both large and small.

- ༀ Skewers/Kebab Sticks – The long-handled metal skewers are good for firm foods. If using wooden skewers, it is essential that the sticks are soaked in cold water for at least 30 minutes to prevent them from catching alight. It is also a good idea to wrap the handling area in a double piece of kitchen foil so that they can be picked up easily.

- ༀ Griddles/hot plates/Barbecue trays – You can cook food on these over the barbecue in the same way as you might use a frying pan or griddle on the hob – super for foods that are too fragile to be placed directly on the grill rack.

- ༀ Wire brush – An essential tool for cleaning the grill rack.

- ༀ Heavy-duty oven gloves – It is a good idea to wear these to protect your hands from the heat. Separate gloves (as opposed to a linked pair) give greater flexibility when handling a very hot grill rack and tools.

Hints & Tips for Perfect Barbecues

∾ Before buying, decide what type of barbecue you want, which fuel you prefer and where it is going to be located.

∾ Make sure that the barbecue is in a stable position, that the smoke will not be swirling around the food or guests, that the area is well lit for visibility and that you have a fire extinguisher or bucket of water nearby, just in case.

∾ Do not use flammable liquids to ignite the barbecue. If necessary, use 'self lighting' briquettes.

∾ Flavours can be introduced by using pre-flavoured coals or sprinkling herbs or spices on top of the coals.

∾ Normally charcoal needs 20–30 minutes' preheating time.

∾ Wood is perhaps the hardest to regulate and is the most unreliable. The wood needs to burn down until a white or grey ash forms on the coals before using. It can also be sprinkled with flavours. Light about 1 hour before cooking.

∾ Gas and electric barbecues are easy to regulate and normally do not need to be preheated.

∾ Never use the barbecue with bare feet and wear an apron to prevent burns to the body.

∾ Be aware when children and pets are around a hot barbecue and never leave a lit or hot one unattended.

∾ Clean the barbecue thoroughly once cool and before using again.

- Choose meat that does not need long slow cooking – use steaks, ribs or chops.

- To help tenderize and impart more flavour, marinate for at least 30 minutes before cooking. As well as a 'wet' marinade, try a 'rub', which consists of a dry mix usually made from a mixture of spice or dried herbs. Rub this into the food's surface and leave for 30 minutes before cooking. Marinades are also good for whole fish as well as fillets, kebabs, poultry, fruits and vegetables such as peppers, aubergines and courgettes. When ready to cook, remove the marinated food and allow any excess marinade to drip back into the dish rather than on the hot coals. If liked, brush the food lightly with extra marinade during cooking.

- Ensure that poultry and pork are thoroughly cooked. Remember that boneless cuts are quicker to cook than, say, drumsticks.

- Never leave raw foods, especially meats, poultry or salads, in direct sunlight or a warm place for longer than a few minutes. Keep covered in a cool place until ready to serve.

- Use separate utensils, especially pastry brushes, knives and boards, for raw and cooked foods in order to avoid cross contamination.

- Prepare as much as possible ahead of time. This will speed up the cooking once you are ready to start cooking.

- If food is cooking too quickly move it away from the centre, towards the edge of the grill.

- The best way of checking the heat of the charcoal is with the hand. Place your hand above the heat – the longer you can keep it there the cooler the barbecue: 2 seconds = hot, 3–4 seconds = medium hot and 5–6 seconds = low heat

Note: in the recipes in this book, 'prepare the barbecue' means 'prepare and light the barbecue' – it will depend on which fuel you are using as to how long before cooking you will need to do this. If a recipe asks you to 'prepare a covered' barbecue, this means a kettle barbecue or some sort of barbecue with a hood, to enable you to trap the rising heat.

Essentials

Butters, Coatings & Marinades

A dded flavour, texture and succulence can be added with the use of various coatings – whether dry coatings, flavoured butters or delicious marinades that are left on for some time before the food is cooked. Why not have a go and experiment with your own flavours?

Dry Coatings

Dry mixtures of breadcrumbs, herbs and spices add flavour and texture to barbecued food. They can also protect the food from the harsh heat of the grill, resulting in a more subtle, grilled flavour. A simple coating of breadcrumbs can keep food moist inside while creating a crisp and crunchy outside. Food coated in a blend of fresh herbs and spices can be left to marinate before cooking. Dry coatings best suit thinner portions that cook quickly so the coatings don't burn. Partially cook longer-cooking foods before coating and grilling them. Try these three different mixtures:

For 2 Fish Fillets

grated rind of 1 lemon or 1 lime
2 tbsp freshly chopped coriander
1 tbsp chopped chervil
sea salt and freshly ground
   black pepper to taste

For 4 Chicken Breast Fillets

3 tbsp fresh white breadcrumbs
1 small red chilli pepper, seeds removed and chopped
2 tbsp chopped basil leaves
grated rind of 1 lime
1 clove garlic, finely chopped
sea salt and freshly ground black pepper to taste

For 450 g/1 lb Beef, Lamb or Pork

1 tsp Chinese five-spice powder
1 tsp sea salt
1 tsp freshly ground black pepper
2 tbsp freshly chopped coriander leaves
1 small red chilli pepper, seeded and chopped

Follow these steps when using any dry coating mixture:

1. Brush the food with oil and coat in the prepared mixture.
2. Cook on a preheated oiled barbecue, griddle or grill.

Flavoured Butters

A slice of flavoured butter melting on a hot-from-the-grill piece of fish, chicken, meat or vegetable is a quick and tasty additional seasoning. They can be made up to 3–4 days ahead of time or frozen or up to 2 months. Flavoured butters are rolled into logs, then sliced, scooped or piped onto cooked foods. They are also a delicious spread for warm grilled bread.

For 450 g/1 lb Fish or Seafood

Option 1
125 g/4 oz softened butter
grated rind and juice of 1 lime

Option 2
125 g/4 oz softened butter
2 tbsp freshly chopped coriander
1 tbsp chopped chervil
1 clove garlic, chopped
juice of 1 lemon

For 450 g/1 lb Beef, Lamb or Pork

Option 1
125 g/4 oz softened butter
2 tsp chopped rosemary
1 small red chilli pepper, seeded and finely chopped
freshly ground black pepper

Essentials

Option 2

125 g/4 oz softened butter
2 cloves garlic, chopped
2 spring onions, finely chopped
freshly ground black pepper

For 450 g/1 lb Chicken

Option 1

125 g/4 oz softened butter
2 canned anchovy fillets,
    drained and mashed
juice of 1 lemon
freshly ground black pepper

Option 2

125 g/4 oz softened butter
2 cloves garlic, finely chopped
1 small green chilli pepper, seeded
    and finely chopped
grated rind and juice of 1 lime

Follow these steps when using any of the
flavoured butter options:

1. Beat the butter until soft, with a spoon
   or mixer..
2. Add the flavourings and mix well.
3. Spoon onto a piece of clingfilm and shape
   into a log.
4. Remove the clingfilm and slice into rounds
   to serve.

Marinades

One of the easiest ways to add flavour and
succulence to food before barbecuing is to
marinate. Foods can be marinated for a few
minutes or up to several hours, and even
overnight. The longer the marinating time, the
stronger the flavour will be, so don't marinate
delicately flavoured foods like fish for too long –
30 minutes is usually sufficient.

At least 3 hours is recommended for marinating
skinless chicken (12 hours with skin), and
to really tenderize beef or lamb, 8 hours to
overnight is ideal. Food should be refrigerated

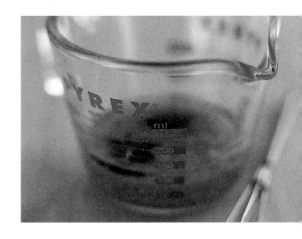

while marinating but brought back to room temperature before cooking to achieve optimum flavour.

Leftover marinades can be brushed over the food while it is cooking, or heated and served as a sauce, but make sure alwaysto boil the marinade for at least 1 minute before serving.

Because many marinades have an acid-based ingredient, it is best to marinate food in shallow nonmetallic dishes. Heavy-duty plastic bags are also good for marinating foods.

Prepared marinades can be stored in screw-top jars in the refrigerator for up to two weeks.

Sweet Chilli Marinade
For 450 g/1 lb fish, seafood or chicken
2 tbsp vegetable oil
2 tbsp Thai sweet chilli sauce
2 tbsp lemon or lime juice
3 cloves garlic, chopped
3 tsp grated ginger
1 tbsp freshly chopped coriander
salt and pepper to taste

Thai Lime Marinade
For 900 g/2 lb prawns, baby octopus or fish fillets
250 ml/8 fl oz coconut milk
50 ml/2 fl oz olive oil
50 ml/2 fl oz lime juice
2 tbsp finely grated lime zest
1 tbsp finely grated fresh ginger
2 cloves garlic, crushed
2 small red chilli peppers, thinly sliced
2 tbsp packed brown sugar
1 tbsp fish sauce

Soy and Basil Marinade
For 450 g/1 lb beef, lamb or pork
2 tbsp vegetable oil
1 tbsp chopped basil leaves
3 tbsp soy sauce
grated rind of 1 lemon
3 cloves garlic, chopped
salt and pepper to taste

Ginger Marinade
For 450 g/1 lb vegetables
2 tbsp vegetable oil
2 tsp sesame oil
2 cloves garlic, chopped
2 tsp grated ginger
salt and pepper to taste

Sweet and Sour Marinade
For 1.5 Kg/3 lb pork (spareribs, loin or chops)
1 small pineapple, peeled, cut lengthwise into quarters, cored and thinly sliced (or 750 g/1½ lb tinned pineapple)
125 ml/4 fl oz pineapple juice
50 ml/2 fl oz lime juice

Essentials

2 cloves crushed garlic
1 small red chilli pepper, finely chopped
60 g/2 oz packed brown sugar

Grapefruit and Brandy Marinade
For 1.1 kg/2¼ lb lamb
125 ml/4 fl oz grapefruit juice
1 grapefruit, peeled, pith removed, cut into
    segments and seeded
75 g/3 oz honey
50 ml/2 fl oz brandy
50 ml/2 fl oz dry white wine
2 tbsp fresh thyme leaves
freshly ground pepper

Cranberry Marinade
For 900 g/2 lb poultry or fish
185 g/6½ oz cranberries
2 tbsp red wine vinegar
50 ml/2 fl oz olive oil
2 tbsp finely grated orange zest
2 cinnamon sticks
1 tbsp finely grated fresh ginger
3 tbsp packed brown sugar

Raspberry Marinade
For 700 g/1½ lb poultry or fish
225 g/8 oz raspberries
50 ml/2 fl oz raspberry vinegar
125 ml/4 fl oz olive oil
10 g/¼ oz fresh tarragon leaves
freshly ground pepper

Follow these steps when using any of the
marinade options:

1. Place the marinade ingredients in a screw-top
   jar or jug and mix well.
2. Place the fish, chicken, meat or vegetables
   into a shallow non metallic dish.
3. Pour or brush the marinade over the food.
   Cover and refrigerate.
4. Drain, then cook on the heated barbecue or
   grill, basting regularly with leftover marinade.

Hygiene in the Kitchen

It is well worth remembering that many foods can carry some form of bacteria. In most cases, the worst it will lead to is a bout of food poisoning or gastroenteritis, although for certain groups this can be more serious. The risk can be reduced or eliminated by good food hygiene and proper cooking.

Be wary of food that is past its sell-by date or its use-by date. When buying food, use the eyes and nose. If the food looks tired, limp or a bad colour or it has a rank, acrid or simply bad smell, do not buy or eat it under any circumstances.

Regularly clean, defrost and clear out the refrigerator or freezer – it is worth checking the packaging to see exactly how long each product is safe to freeze.

Dish cloths and tea towels must be washed and changed regularly. Ideally use disposable cloths which should be replaced on a daily basis. More durable cloths should be left to soak in bleach, then washed in the washing machine on a boil wash. Always keep your hands, cooking utensils and food preparation surfaces clean and never allow pets to climb on to any work surfaces.

Buying

Avoid bulk buying where possible, especially fresh produce such as meat, poultry, fish, fruit and vegetables unless buying for the freezer. Fresh foods lose their nutritional value rapidly so buying a little at a time minimises loss of nutrients. It also eliminates a packed refrigerator which reduces the effectiveness of the refrigeration process.

Essentials

When buying frozen foods, ensure that they are not heavily iced on the outside. Place in the freezer as soon as possible after purchase.

Preparation

Make sure that all work surfaces and utensils are clean and dry. Separate chopping boards should be used for raw and cooked meats, fish and vegetables. It is worth washing all fruits and vegetables regardless of whether they are going to be eaten raw or lightly cooked. Do not reheat food more than once.

All poultry must be thoroughly thawed before cooking. Leave the food in the refrigerator until it is completely thawed. Once defrosted, the chicken should be cooked as soon as possible. The only time food can be refrozen is when the food has been thoroughly thawed then cooked. Once the food has cooled then it can be frozen again for one month.

All poultry and game (except for duck) must be cooked thoroughly. When cooked the juices will run clear. Other meats, like minced meat and pork should be cooked right the way through. Fish should turn opaque, be firm in texture and break easily into large flakes.

Storing, Refrigerating and Freezing

Meat, poultry, fish, seafood and dairy products should all be refrigerated. The temperature of the refrigerator should be between 1–5°C/34–41°F while the freezer temperature should not rise above -18°C/-0.4°F. When refrigerating cooked food, allow it to cool down completely before refrigerating. Hot food will raise the temperature of the refrigerator and possibly affect or spoil other food stored in it.

Food within the refrigerator and freezer should always be covered. Raw and cooked food should be stored in separate parts of the refrigerator. Cooked food should be kept on the top shelves of the refrigerator, while raw meat, poultry and fish should be placed on bottom shelves to avoid drips and cross-contamination.

High-Risk Foods

Certain foods may carry risks to people who are considered vulnerable such as the elderly, the ill, pregnant women, babies and those suffering from a recurring illness. It is advisable to avoid those foods which belong to a higher-risk category.

There is a slight chance that some eggs carry the bacteria salmonella. Cook the eggs until both the yolk and the white are firm to eliminate this risk. Sauces including Hollandaise, mayonnaise, mousses, soufflés and meringues all use raw or lightly cooked eggs, as do custard-based dishes, ice creams and sorbets. These are all considered high-risk foods to the vulnerable groups mentioned above. Certain meats and poultry also carry the potential risk of salmonella and so should be cooked thoroughly until the juices run clear and there is no pinkness left. Unpasteurised products such as milk, cheese (especially soft cheese), pâté, meat (both raw and cooked) all have the potential risk of listeria and should be avoided.

When buying seafood, buy from a reputable source. Fish should have bright clear eyes, shiny skin and bright pink or red gills. The fish should feel stiff to the touch, with a slight smell of sea air and iodine. The flesh of fish steaks and fillets should be translucent with no signs of discolouration. Avoid any molluscs that are open or do not close when tapped lightly. Univalves such as cockles or winkles should withdraw into their shells when lightly prodded. Squid and octopus should have firm flesh and a pleasant sea smell.

Care is required when freezing seafood. It is imperative to check whether the fish has been frozen before. If it has been, then it should not be frozen again under any circumstances.

Essentials

Nutrition

A healthy and well-balanced diet is the body's primary energy source. In children, it constitutes the building blocks for future health as well as providing lots of energy. In adults, it encourages self-healing and regeneration within the body. A well-balanced diet will provide the body with all the essential nutrients it needs. This can be achieved by eating a variety of foods, demonstrated in the pyramid below:

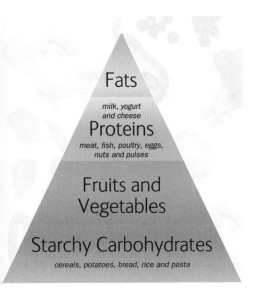

Fats

Fats fall into two categories: saturated and unsaturated fats. It is very important that a healthy balance is achieved within the diet. Fats are an essential part of the diet and a source of energy and provide essential fatty acids and fat–soluble vitamins. The right balance of fats should boost the body's immunity to infection and keep muscles, nerves and arteries in good condition. Saturated fats are of animal origin and are hard when stored at room temperature. They can be found in dairy produce, meat, eggs, margarines and hard, white cooking fat (lard) as well as in manufactured products such as pies, biscuits and cakes. A high intake of saturated fat over many years has been proven to increase heart disease and high blood cholesterol levels and often leads to weight gain. The aim of a healthy diet is to keep the fat content low in the foods that we eat. Lowering the amount of saturated fat that we consume is very important, but this does not mean that it is good to consume lots of other types of fat.

There are two kinds of unsaturated fats: polyunsaturated fats and monounsaturated fats. Polyunsaturated fats include the following oils: safflower oil, soybean oil, corn oil and sesame oil. Within the polyunsaturated group are Omega oils. The Omega-3 oils are of significant interest because they have been found to be particularly beneficial to coronary health and can encourage brain growth and development. Omega-3 oils are derived from oily fish such as salmon, mackerel, herring, pilchards and sardines. It is recommended that we should eat these types of fish at least once a week. However, for those who do not eat fish or who are vegetarians, liver oil supplements are available in most supermarkets and health shops. It is suggested that these supplements should be taken on a daily basis. The most popular oils that are high in monounsaturates are olive oil, sunflower oil and peanut oil. The Mediterranean diet, which is based on foods high in monounsaturated fats, is recommended for heart health. Also, monounsaturated fats are known to help reduce the levels of LDL (the bad) cholesterol.

Proteins

Composed of amino acids (proteins' building bricks), proteins perform a wide variety of functions for the body, including supplying energy and building and repairing tissue. Good sources of proteins are eggs, milk, yogurt, cheese, meat, fish, poultry, nuts and pulses. (See the second level of the pyramid.) Some of these foods, however, contain saturated fats. For a nutritional balance, eat generous amounts of soya beans, lentils, peas and nuts.

Fruits and Vegetables

Not only are fruits and vegetables the most visually appealing foods, but they are extremely good for us, providing vital vitamins and minerals essential for growth, repair and protection in the human body. Fruits and vegetables are low in calories and are responsible for regulating the body's metabolic processes and controlling the composition of its fluids and cells.

Essentials

Minerals

❧ Calcium – Important for healthy bones and teeth, nerve transmission, muscle contraction, blood clotting and hormone function. Calcium promotes a healthy heart, improves skin, relieves aching muscles and bones, maintains the correct acid-alkaline balance and reduces menstrual cramps. Good sources are dairy products, small bones of small fish, nuts, pulses, fortified white flours, breads and green, leafy vegetables.

❧ Chromium – Part of the glucose tolerance factor, chromium balances blood sugar levels, helps to normalise hunger and reduce cravings, improves lifespan, helps protect DNA and is essential for heart function. Good sources are brewer's yeast, wholemeal bread, rye bread, oysters, potatoes, green peppers, butter and parsnips.

❧ Iodine – Important for thyroid hormones and for normal development. Good sources of iodine are seafood, seaweed, milk and dairy products.

❧ Iron – As a component of haemoglobin, iron carries oxygen around the body. It is vital for normal growth and development. Good sources are liver, corned beef, red meat, fortified breakfast cereals, pulses, green, leafy vegetables, egg yolk and cocoa and cocoa products.

❧ Magnesium – Important for efficient functioning of metabolic enzymes and development of the skeleton. Magnesium promotes healthy muscles by helping them to relax and is therefore good for PMS. It is also important for heart muscles and the nervous system. Good sources are nuts, green vegetables, meat, cereals, milk and yogurt.

- Phosphorus – Forms and maintains bones and teeth, builds muscle tissue, helps maintain the body's pH and aids metabolism and energy production. Phosphorus is present in almost all foods.

- Potassium – Enables nutrients to move into cells, while waste products move out; promotes healthy nerves and muscles; maintains fluid balance in the body; helps secretion of insulin for blood sugar control to produce constant energy; relaxes muscles; maintains heart functioning and stimulates gut movement to encourage proper elimination. Good sources are fruit, vegetables, milk and bread.

- Selenium – Antioxidant properties help to protect against free radicals and carcinogens. Selenium reduces inflammation, stimulates the immune system to fight infections, promotes a healthy heart and helps vitamin E's action. It is also required for the male reproductive system and is needed for metabolism. Good sources are tuna, liver, kidney, meat, eggs, cereals, nuts and dairy products.

- Sodium – Helps to control body fluid and balance, preventing dehydration. Sodium is involved in muscle and nerve function and helps move nutrients into cells. All foods are good sources, but pickled and salted foods are richest in sodium.

- Zinc – Important for metabolism and the healing of wounds. It also aids ability to cope with stress, promotes a healthy nervous system and brain, especially in the growing foetus, aids bones and teeth formation and is essential for constant energy. Good sources are liver, meat, pulses, wholegrain cereals, nuts and oysters.

Vitamins

- **Vitamin A** – Important for cell growth and development and for the formation of visual pigments in the eye. Found in liver, meat, whole milk, red and yellow fruits and carrots.

- **Vitamin B1** – Important in releasing energy from carbohydrate-containing foods. Good sources are yeast and yeast products, bread, fortified breakfast cereals and potatoes.

- **Vitamin B2** – Important for metabolism of proteins, fats and carbohydrates. Found in meat, yeast extract, fortified cereals and milk.

- **Vitamin B3** – Helps the metabolism of food into energy. Sources are milk and milk products, fortified breakfast cereals, pulses, meat, poultry and eggs.

- **Vitamin B5** – Important for the metabolism of food and energy production. All foods are good sources, but especially fortified breakfast cereals, wholegrain bread and dairy products.

- **Vitamin B6** – Important for metabolism of protein and fat. Vitamin B6 may also be involved with the regulation of sex hormones. Good sources are liver, fish, pork, soya beans and peanuts.

- **Vitamin B12** – Important for the production of red blood cells and DNA. It is vital for growth and the nervous system. Good sources are meat, fish, eggs, poultry and milk.

- **Biotin** – Important for metabolism of fatty acids. Good sources of biotin are liver, kidney, eggs and nuts. Micro-organisms also manufacture this vitamin in the gut.

- Vitamin C – Important for healing wounds and the formation of collagen, which keeps skin and bones strong. It is an important antioxidant. Sources are fruits and vegetables.

- Vitamin D – Important for absorption of calcium to build bone strength. Sources are oily fish, eggs, whole milk and milk products, margarine, and sunlight – vitamin D is made in the skin.

- Vitamin E – Important as an antioxidant vitamin, helping to protect cell membranes from damage. Good sources are vegetable oils, margarines, seeds, nuts and green vegetables.

- Folic Acid – Critical during pregnancy for the development of foetus brain and nerves. It is essential for brain and nerve function and is needed for protein and red blood cell formation. Sources are wholegrain cereals, fortified cereals, green, leafy vegetables, oranges and liver.

- Vitamin K – Important for controlling blood clotting. Sources are cauliflower, Brussels sprouts, lettuce, cabbage, beans, broccoli, peas, asparagus, potatoes, corn oil, tomatoes and milk.

Carbohydrates

Carbohydrates come in two basic forms: starch and sugar carbohydrates. Starch carbohydrates, also known as complex carbohydrates, include cereals, potatoes, breads, rice and pasta. (See the fourth level of the pyramid). Eating wholegrain varieties also provides fibre, beneficial in preventing bowel cancer, and controlling cholesterol weight. Sugar carbohydrates, known as fast-release carbohydrates (because of the quick fix of energy they give), include sugar and sugar-sweetened products such as jams and syrups. Milk provides lactose, which is milk sugar, and fruits provide fructose, which is fruit sugar.

Essentials

Fish & Seafood

For those used to burgers and sausages, fish and seafood may not spring to mind as classic barbecue fare, but they actually lend themselves beautifully to the coals and evoke heady Mediterranean afternoons. Try some classic Barbecued Fish Kebabs or broaden your horizons with a more delicate Cod with Fennel & Cardamom, steamed inside a cosy little parcel ready to be opened for your delighted guests.

Gingered Cod Steaks

Serves 4

2.5 cm/1 inch piece fresh
root ginger, peeled
4 spring onions
2 tsp freshly chopped parsley
1 tbsp soft brown sugar
4 x 175 g/6 oz thick cod steaks
salt and freshly ground
black pepper
25 g/1 oz butter
salad or freshly cooked vegetables,
to serve

Prepare the barbecue, or preheat the grill and line the grill rack with a layer of tinfoil. Coarsely grate the piece of ginger. Trim the spring onions and cut into thin strips.

Mix the spring onions, ginger, chopped parsley and sugar. Add 1 tablespoon of water.

Wipe the fish steaks. Season to taste with salt and pepper. Place on to 4 separate 20.5 x 20.5 cm/8 x 8 inch kitchen foil squares.

Carefully spoon the spring onions and ginger mixture over the fish. Cut the butter into small cubes and place over the fish.

Loosely fold the foil over the steaks to enclose the fish and to make a parcel. Place on the barbecue or under the preheated grill and cook for 10–15 minutes or until cooked and the flesh has turned opaque.

Place the fish parcels on individual serving plates. Serve immediately with the salad or freshly cooked vegetables.

Cod with Fennel & Cardamom

Serves 4

1 garlic clove, peeled
and crushed

finely grated rind of 1 lemon

1 tsp lemon juice

1 tbsp olive oil

1 fennel bulb

1 tbsp cardamom pods

salt and freshly ground
black pepper

4 x 175 g/6 oz thick
cod fillets

Prepare the barbecue or preheat the oven to 190°C/375°F/Gas Mark 5. Place the garlic in a small bowl with the lemon rind, juice and olive oil and stir well. Cover and leave to infuse for at least 30 minutes. Stir well before using.

Trim the fennel bulb, thinly slice and place in a bowl.

Place the cardamom pods in a pestle and mortar and lightly pound to crack the pods. Alternatively place in a polythene bag and pound gently with a rolling pin. Add the crushed cardamom to the fennel slices.

Season the fish with salt and pepper and place on to 4 separate 20.5 x 20.5 cm/8 x 8 inch parchment paper squares.

Spoon the fennel mixture over the fish and drizzle with the infused oil. If cooking on the barbecue, place the parcels on squares of kitchen foil and fold up around the paper for protection; place on the barbecue. If cooking on the oven, place the paper parcels on a baking sheet and put into the preheated oven. Cook on the barbecue for 12–15 minutes, or in the oven for 8–10 minutes, or until cooked. Serve immediately in the paper parcels.

Barbecued Fish Kebabs

Serves 4

at least 4 wooden skewers
450 g/1 lb herring or mackerel fillets,
cut into chunks
2 small red onions, peeled and
quartered
16 cherry tomatoes
salt and freshly ground
black pepper
salad or couscous, to serve

For the sauce

150 ml/¼ pint fish stock
5 tbsp tomato ketchup
2 tbsp Worcestershire sauce
2 tbsp wine vinegar
2 tbsp brown sugar
2 drops Tabasco
2 tbsp tomato purée

Soak the skewers in cold water for 30 minutes to prevent them from catching alight during cooking, then drain.

Meanwhile, prepare the barbecue. Or, if using a grill, line the rack with a single layer of kitchen foil and, 2 minutes before use, preheat the grill at a high temperature.

Meanwhile, prepare the sauce. Add the fish stock, tomato ketchup, Worcestershire sauce, vinegar, sugar, Tabasco and tomato purée to a small saucepan. Stir well and leave to simmer for 5 minutes.

When ready to cook, drain the skewers, if necessary, then thread the fish chunks, the quartered red onions and the cherry tomatoes alternately on to the skewers.

Season the kebabs to taste with salt and pepper and brush with the sauce. Cook on the barbecue or under the preheated grill for 8–10 minutes, basting with the sauce occasionally during cooking. Turn the kebabs often to ensure that they are cooked thoroughly and evenly on all sides. Serve immediately with salad or couscous.

Barbecued Salmon with Wasabi Butter

Serves 4

125 g/4 oz butter, softened
2 tsp wasabi paste
grated rind of 1 lime
1 tbsp lime juice
½ tsp freshly ground
black pepper
4 salmon steaks,
approx. 6 oz/175 g each
2 tbsp vegetable oil
fresh coriander, to garnish

For crispy fried potatoes

3 potatoes, peeled and
very thinly sliced
125 ml/4 fl oz vegetable oil, for frying

Prepare the barbecue. Using a sharp knife, cut the bone away from each salmon steak to create fillets. Repeat with the remaining salmon steaks. Remove the skin.

In a mixing bowl, beat the butter until soft. Add the wasabi paste, rind, juice and pepper and mix until well combined. Refrigerate until firm. Brush the salmon with oil. On the barbecue or in a grill pan, cook the salmon 2–3 minutes each side (the salmon should remain pink in the centre), then allow to stand 5 minutes.

Place onto serving plates. Using a teaspoon or melon baller, scoop the wasabi butter onto the salmon pieces. Serve with crispy fried potatoes and garnish with fresh coriander.

To make crispy fried potatoes, pat the potato dry with kitchen towel. On a barbecue tray or In a frying pan, heat oil over medium heat and, working in batches, fry the potato slices for about 2 minutes, or until golden and crisp. Remove with a slotted spoon and drain on kitchen towel.

Seared Tuna with Pernod & Thyme

Serves 4

4 tuna or swordfish steaks
salt and freshly ground black pepper
3 tbsp Pernod
1 tbsp olive oil
zest and juice of 1 lime
2 tsp fresh thyme leaves
4 sun-dried tomatoes

To serve

freshly cooked mixed rice (optional)
tossed green salad

Wipe the fish steaks with a damp cloth or dampened kitchen paper. Season both sides of the fish to taste with salt and pepper, then place in a shallow bowl and reserve.

Mix together the Pernod, olive oil, lime zest and juice with the fresh thyme leaves.

Finely chop the sun-dried tomatoes and add to the Pernod mixture. Pour the mixture over the fish and chill in the refrigerator for about 2 hours, spooning the marinade occasionally over the fish.

Meanwhile prepare the barbecue, or when ready to cook, heat a griddle or heavy-based frying pan. Drain the fish, reserving the marinade. Cook the fish for 3–4 minutes on each side for a steak that is still slightly pink in the middle. Or, if liked, cook the fish for 1–2 minutes longer on each side if you prefer your fish cooked through. If you want to avoid the marinade elements dropping through the barbecue rack, you could try using a griddle plate or barbecue tray over the barbecue. If doing this remember that the tuna will take at least twice as long than if being cooked straight on the barbecue.

Place the remaining marinade in a small saucepan and bring to the boil. Pour the marinade over the fish and serve immediately, with the mixed rice, if using, and salad.

Seared Tuna with Italian Salsa

Serves 4

4 x 175 g/6 oz tuna or swordfish steaks
salt and freshly ground black pepper
3 tbsp Pernod
2 tbsp olive oil
zest and juice of 1 lemon
2 tsp fresh thyme leaves
2 tsp fennel seeds, lightly roasted
4 sun-dried tomatoes, chopped
1 tsp dried chilli flakes
assorted salad leaves, to serve

For the salsa

1 white onion, peeled and finely chopped
2 tomatoes, deseeded and sliced
2 tbsp freshly shredded basil leaves
1 red chilli, deseeded and finely sliced
3 tbsp extra-virgin olive oil
2 tsp balsamic vinegar
1 tsp caster sugar

Wipe the fish and season lightly with salt and pepper, then place in a shallow dish. Mix together the Pernod, olive oil, lemon zest and juice, thyme, fennel seeds, sun-dried tomatoes and chilli flakes and pour over the fish. Cover lightly and leave to marinate in a cool place for 1–2 hours, occasionally spooning the marinade over the fish.

Meanwhile, prepare the barbecue. Mix all the salsa ingredients together in a small bowl. Season to taste with salt and pepper, then cover and leave for about 30 minutes to marinate.

If not using the barbecue, when ready to cook, lightly oil a griddle pan and heat until very hot. Drain the fish, reserving the marinade. Cook the fish for 3–4 minutes on each side, taking care not to overcook them – the tuna steaks should be a little pink inside. If you want to avoid the marinade elements dropping through the barbecue rack, you could try using a griddle plate or barbecue tray on the barbecue. Remember that the tuna will take at least twice as long than if being cooked straight on the barbecue.

Pour any remaining marinade into a small saucepan, bring to the boil and boil for 1 minute. Serve the steaks hot with the marinade, chilled salsa and a few assorted salad leaves.

Citrus Monkfish Kebabs

Serves 4

For the marinade

1 tbsp sunflower oil
finely grated rind and juice of 1 lime
1 tbsp lemon juice
1 sprig freshly chopped rosemary
1 tbsp whole-grain mustard
1 garlic clove, peeled
and crushed
salt and freshly ground black pepper

For the kebabs

8 wooden skewers
450 g/1 lb monkfish tail
8 raw tiger prawns
1 small green courgette, trimmed
and sliced
4 tbsp of crème fraîche

Prepare the barbecue, or line the grill rack with foil and preheat the grill 2 minutes before using. Mix all the marinade ingredients together in a small bowl and reserve.

Using a sharp knife, cut down both sides of the monkfish tail. Remove the bone and discard. Cut away and discard any skin, then cut the monkfish into bite-size cubes.

Peel the prawns, leaving the tails intact and remove the thin black vein that runs down the back of each prawn. Place the fish and prans in a shallow dish.

Pour the marinade, reserving 2 tablespoons, over the fish and prawns. Cover lightly and leave to marinate in the refrigerator for 30 minutes. Spoon the marinade over the fish and prawns occasionally during this time. Soak the skewers in cold water for 30 minutes, then drain.

Thread the cubes of fish, prawns and courgettes on to the drained skewers. Place on the barbecue or arrange on the grill rack then place under the preheated grill, and cook for 5–7 minutes, or until cooked thoroughly and the prawns have turned pink. Occasionally brush with the remaining marinade and turn the kebabs during cooking.

Mix the reserved marinade with the crème fraîche and serve as a dip with the kebabs.

Prawn, Lime & Chilli Pepper Skewers

Serves 3–4

12 king prawns
4 tbsp vegetable oil
freshly ground black pepper
3 tbsp lime juice
2 tsp grated ginger
2 cloves garlic, finely chopped
12 bamboo skewers
2 limes, cut into 6 wedges each
12 small red chilli peppers
2 red onions, cut into 6 wedges each
40 g/1½ oz mixed salad greens,
for serving

Peel the prawns, leaving the tails on. Using a sharp knife, remove the black vein along the back of the prawns. Place the prawns in a shallow nonmetallic dish.

In a small bowl, combine 2 tablespoons of the oil, some black pepper, the lime juice, ginger, and garlic, mix well and pour over the prawns. Cover the dish with clingfilm and refrigerate for 1 hour.

Meanwhile, prepare the barbecue or line the grill rack with foil and preheat the grill 2 minutes before using. Soak the bamboo skewers in cold water for 30 minutes, then drain.

Remove the prawns from the marinade. Thread a prawn, lime wedge, chilli pepper and red onion wedge onto each skewer. Away from the hot coals, brush the barbecue grill (or the grill rack) with the remaining oil. Cook the skewers for 2–3 minutes on each side, or until the prawns change colour. Remove from the grill and serve warm with salad greens.

Sardines with Redcurrants

Serves 4

2 tbsp redcurrant jelly
finely grated rind of 1 lime
2 tbsp medium dry sherry
450 g/1 lb fresh sardines, cleaned,
and heads removed if preferred
sea salt and freshly ground
black pepper
lime wedges, to garnish

To serve

fresh redcurrants
fresh green salad

Prepare the barbecue, or preheat the grill and line the grill rack with kitchen foil 2–3 minutes before cooking.

Warm the redcurrant jelly in a bowl standing over a pan of gently simmering water and stir until smooth. Add the lime rind and sherry to the bowl and stir well until blended.

Lightly rinse the sardines and pat dry with absorbent kitchen paper. Place on a chopping board and with a sharp knife make several diagonal cuts across the flesh of each fish. Season the sardines inside the cavities with salt and pepper.

Gently brush the warm marinade over the skin and inside the cavities of the sardines. Place on the barbecue, or on the grill rack under the preheated grill, and cook for 8–10 minutes, or until the fish are cooked. Carefully turn the sardines over at least once during grilling. Baste occasionally with the remaining redcurrant and lime marinade.

Garnish with the redcurrants. Serve immediately with the salad and lime wedges.

Sardines in Vine Leaves

Serves 4

8–16 vine leaves in brine, drained
2 spring onions
6 tbsp olive oil
2 tbsp lime juice
2 tbsp freshly chopped oregano
1 tsp mustard powder
salt and freshly ground black pepper
8 sardines, cleaned
8 bay leaves
8 sprigs of fresh dill

To garnish
lime wedges
sprigs of fresh dill

To serve
olive salad
crusty bread

Prepare the barbecue, or preheat the grill and line the grill rack with kitchen foil just before cooking. Cut 8 pieces of string about 25.5 cm/10 inches long, and leave to soak in cold water for about 10 minutes. Cover the vine leaves in almost boiling water. Leave for 20 minutes, then drain and rinse thoroughly. Pat the vine leaves dry with absorbent kitchen paper.

Trim the spring onions and finely chop, then place into a small bowl. With a balloon whisk beat in the olive oil, lime juice, oregano, mustard powder and season to taste with salt and pepper. Cover with clingfilm and leave in the refrigerator, until required. Stir the mixture before using.

Prepare the sardines, by making 2 slashes on both sides of each fish and brush with a little of the lime juice mixture. Place a bay leaf and a dill sprig inside each sardine cavity and wrap with 1–2 vine leaves, depending on size. Brush with the lime mixture and tie the vine leaves in place with string.

Cook the fish on the barbecue, or under a medium hot grill, for 4–5 minutes on each side, brushing with a little more of the lime mixture if necessary. Leave the fish to rest, unwrap and discard the vine leaves. Garnish with lime wedges and sprigs of fresh dill and serve with the remaining lime mixture, olive salad and crusty bread.

Red Mullet with Orange & Anchovy Sauce

Serves 4

2 oranges
4 x 175 g/6 oz red mullet, cleaned
and descaled
salt and freshly ground
black pepper
4 sprigs of fresh rosemary
1 lemon, sliced
2 tbsp olive oil
2 garlic cloves, peeled
and crushed
6 anchovy fillets in oil, drained and
roughly chopped
2 tsp freshly chopped rosemary
1 tsp lemon juice

Prepare the barbecue, or preheat the grill and line the grill rack with kitchen foil just before cooking.

Peel the oranges with a sharp knife, over a bowl in order to catch the juice. Cut into thin slices and reserve. If necessary, make up the juice to 150 ml/¼ pint with extra juice.

Place the fish on a chopping board and make 2 diagonal slashes across the thickest part of both sides of the fish. Season well, both inside and out, with salt and pepper. Tuck a rosemary sprig and a few lemon slices inside the cavity of each fish.

Brush the fish with a little of the olive oil and then cook on the barbecue or under the preheated grill for 4–5 minutes on each side. The flesh should just fall away from the bone.

Heat the remaining oil in a saucepan and gently fry the garlic and anchovies for 3–4 minutes. Do not allow to brown. Add the chopped rosemary and plenty of black pepper. The anchovies will be salty enough, so do not add any salt.

Stir in the orange slices with their juice and the lemon juice. Simmer gently until heated through. Spoon the sauce over the red mullet and serve immediately.

Salmon Fish Cakes

Serves 4

225 g/8 oz potatoes, peeled
450 g/1 lb salmon fillet, skinned
125 g/4 oz carrot, trimmed
and peeled
2 tbsp grated lemon rind
2–3 tbsp freshly chopped coriander
1 medium egg yolk
salt and freshly ground black pepper
2 tbsp plain white flour
few fine sprays of oil

To serve

prepared tomato sauce
tossed green salad
crusty bread

Prepare the barbecue. Cube the potatoes and cook in lightly salted boiling water for 15 minutes. Drain and mash the potatoes. Place in a mixing bowl and reserve.

Place the salmon in a food processor and blend to form a chunky purée. Add the purée to the potatoes and mix together.

Coarsely grate the carrot and add to the fish with the lemon rind and the coriander.

Add the egg yolk, season to taste with salt and pepper, then gently mix the ingredients together. With damp hands form the mixture into 4 large fish cakes. Coat in the flour and place on a plate. Cover loosely and chill for at least 30 minutes.

When ready to cook, place the fish cakes onto a hot, oiled griddle plate on the barbecue, or in a griddle pan on the hob. Cook on both sides for 3–4 minutes or until the fish is cooked. Add an extra spray of oil if needed during the cooking, but be careful not to let any oil drop onto the hot coals or it will catch alight.

When the fish cakes are cooked, serve immediately with the tomato sauce, green salad and crusty bread.

Tuna Fish Burgers

Serves 8

450 g/1 lb potatoes, peeled and
cut into chunks
50 g/2 oz butter
2 tbsp milk
400 g can tuna in oil
1 spring onion, trimmed and finely
chopped
1 tbsp freshly chopped parsley
salt and freshly ground
black pepper
2 medium eggs, beaten
2 tbsp seasoned plain flour
125 g/4 oz fresh white breadcrumbs
4 tbsp vegetable oil

To serve

4 sesame seed baps
fat chips (optional)
mixed salad
tomato chutney

Place the potatoes in a large saucepan, cover with boiling water and simmer until soft. Drain, then mash with 40 g/1½ oz of the butter and the milk. Turn into a large bowl. Drain the tuna, discarding the oil and flake into the bowl of potato. Stir well to mix.

Add the spring onions and parsley to the mixture and season to taste with salt and pepper. Add 1 tablespoon of the beaten egg to bind the mixture together. Chill in the refrigerator for at least 1 hour. Meanwhile, prepare the barbecue.

Shape the chilled mixture with your hands into 4 large burgers. First, coat the burgers with seasoned flour, then brush them with the remaining beaten egg, allowing any excess to drip back into the bowl. Finally, coat them evenly in the breadcrumbs, pressing the crumbs on with your hands, if necessary.

Place the burgers either directly onto the barbecue or onto a barbecue tray on top – either way, use a little of the oil to avoid sticking. Or, heat a little of the oil in a frying pan and fry the burgers. Cook for 2–3 minutes on each side until golden, adding more oil if necessary. Drain on absorbent kitchen paper, if necessary, and serve hot in baps, with chips, if using, mixed salad and chutney.

Hot Tiger Prawns with Parma Ham

Serves 4

4 thin wooden skewers or
12 cocktail sticks
½ cucumber, peeled if preferred
4 ripe tomatoes
12 raw tiger prawns
6 tbsp olive oil
4 garlic cloves, peeled and crushed
4 tbsp freshly chopped parsley
salt and freshly ground black pepper
6 slices of Parma ham, cut in half
4 slices flat Italian bread
4 tbsp dry white wine

If using the barbecue, soak the wooden skewers for 30 minutes before cooking. Prepare the barbecue, or preheat the oven to 180°C/350°F/Gas Mark 4. Slice the cucumber and tomatoes thinly, then arrange on 4 large plates and reserve. Peel the prawns, leaving the tail shell intact and remove the thin black vein running down the back.

Whisk together 4 tablespoons of the olive oil, garlic and chopped parsley in a small bowl and season to taste with plenty of salt and pepper. Add the prawns to the mixture and stir until they are well coated. Remove the prawns, then wrap each one in a piece of Parma ham and, if cooking in the oven, secure each one with a cocktail stick. If using the barbecue, thread the wrapped prawns carefully onto the skewers so that they will sit on the barbecue more easily.

Place the prepared prawns on the barbecue, or on a lightly oiled baking sheet or dish in the preheated oven. Cook for 3 minutes on the barbecue, or 5 minutes in the oven, turning once. At the same time toast the slices of bread in the oven or on the barbecue.

Remove the prawns from the heat and spoon the wine over the prawns and bread. Return to the barbecue or oven and cook for a further 5 or 10 minutes respectively until piping hot. Carefully remove the skewers or cocktail sticks and arrange 3 prawn rolls on each slice of bread. Place on top of the sliced cucumber and tomatoes and serve immediately.

Scallops & Monkfish Kebabs with Fennel Sauce

Serves 4

4 wooden skewers
700 g/1½ lb monkfish tail
8 large fresh scallops
2 tbsp olive oil
1 garlic clove, peeled
and crushed
freshly ground black pepper
1 fennel bulb, trimmed and
thinly sliced
assorted salad leaves, to serve

For the sauce

2 tbsp fennel seeds
pinch of chilli flakes
4 tbsp olive oil
2 tsp lemon juice
salt and freshly ground
black pepper

Prepare the barbecue, and soak the skewers. Place the monkfish on a chopping board and remove the skin and the bone that runs down the centre of the tail and discard. Lightly rinse and pat dry. Cut the 2 fillets into 12 equal-sized pieces and place in a shallow bowl. Remove the scallops from their shells, if necessary, and clean thoroughly discarding the black vein. Rinse lightly and pat dry. Put in the bowl with the fish.

Blend the 2 tablespoons of olive oil, the crushed garlic and a pinch of black pepper in a small bowl, then pour the mixture over the monkfish and scallops, making sure they are well coated. Cover lightly and leave to marinate in the refrigerator for at least 30 minutes, or longer if time permits. Spoon over the marinade occasionally.

Lightly crush the fennel seeds and chilli in a pestle and mortar. Stir in the 4 tablespoons of olive oil and lemon juice and season with salt and pepper. Cover and leave to infuse for 20 minutes.

Drain the monkfish and scallops, reserving the marinade and thread on to 4 skewers. Place on the hot barbecue or on a griddle pan coated with a fine spray of oil and heated until almost smoking, and cook for 5–6 minutes, turning halfway through and brushing with the marinade throughout. Brush the fennel slices with the fennel sauce and cook on the barbecue or griddle for 1 minute on each side. Serve the fennel, topped with the kebabs and drizzled with the fennel sauce. Serve with a few assorted salad leaves.

Curried Prawn Kebabs

Serves 4–6

4–8 wooden kebab skewers
1 tbsp vegetable oil
1 tsp fennel seeds
1 tsp cumin seeds
1 tsp turmeric
1 tsp chilli powder
1 tsp ground coriander
1 red chilli, deseeded and chopped
5 cm/2 inch piece fresh root ginger,
peeled and grated
2 tbsp lime juice
300 ml/½ pint natural yogurt
350 g/12 oz raw large prawns, peeled
2–3 limes, cut into wedges
salad and Indian-style bread, to serve

Prepare the barbecue, or preheat the grill and line the grill rack with kitchen foil 2–3 minutes before cooking. Soak the skewers in cold water for at least 30 minutes, then drain.

Heat the oil in a wok or frying pan, add the seeds and fry for 30 seconds, or until they pop. Add the turmeric, chilli powder, ground coriander, chopped chilli and grated ginger and fry over a gentle heat for 2 minutes. Stir in the lime juice and cook, stirring, for 30 seconds. Remove from the heat and cool slightly before stirring in the yogurt.

Rinse the prawns and pat dry with absorbent kitchen paper, then place in a shallow dish large enough for the prawns to lie in a single layer. Pour the spicy yogurt over the prawns, cover lightly and leave to marinate in the refrigerator for at least 30 minutes, turning the prawns over a couple of times.

Drain the prawns, reserving the marinade, and thread them with the lime wedges onto the drained skewers. Cook on the barbecue for 4–5 minutes or under the grill for 6–8 minutes, or until cooked, turning the prawns over occasionally and brushing with a little of the reserved marinade. Move to the side of the barbecue or turn the heat down if the prawns are cooking too quickly and beginning to burn. Serve with salad and bread.

Mixed Seafood Skewers

Serves 4

12 bamboo skewers
225 g/8 oz king prawns
225 g/8 oz scallops, cleaned
350 g/12 oz white fish fillets, cut into
4-cm/1½-inch cubes
4 tbsp groundnut oil, divided in half
½ onion, coarsely chopped
2 cloves garlic
2 tsp grated ginger
2 stems lemongrass (white section
only), chopped
1 tsp shrimp paste
4 tbsp soy sauce
1 tsp chilli oil
1 tsp sesame oil
25 g/1 oz mizuna leaves, to serve

Prepare the barbecue, or preheat the grill and line the grill rack with kitchen foil 2–3 minutes before cooking. Soak the bamboo skewers in cold water for 30 minutes, then drain.

Peel the prawns, leaving the tails on. Using a sharp knife, remove the black vein along the back of the prawns.

Pat the prawns, scallops and fish dry with kitchen towel and thread alternately onto the skewers. Brush the seafood skewers with 2 tablespoons of the groundnut oil, then place into a shallow nonmetallic dish.

In a food processor, combine the onion, garlic, ginger, lemongrass, shrimp paste, remaining groundnut oil, 1 tablespoon of the soy sauce, the chilli oil and sesame oil and process for about 30 seconds, until the mixture becomes a smooth paste.

Brush the seafood with the spice paste, then cover the dish with clingfilm and refrigerate for 30 minutes. On the barbecue or under the grill, cook the skewers for 3–4 minutes each side, or until the seafood changes colour. Remove from the grill.

Serve warm with the remaining soy sauce as a dipping sauce and the mizuna leaves.

Fish Steaks with Sake

Serves 4

800 g/1¾ lb fish, or 4 fish steaks, approx. 200 g/7 oz each (choose any fish with firm, white flesh, such as monkfish, sea bass, grouper, halibut, coley or cod)
2 tbsp vegetable oil
25 ml/1 fl oz sake
juice and grated rind of 1 lime
2 tsp sea salt
1 tsp freshly ground black pepper
50 g/2 oz baby spinach leaves, to serve
2 tbsp additional grated lime rind, to serve

Prepare the barbecue, or preheat the grill and line the grill rack with kitchen foil 2–3 minutes before cooking. If using monkfish, cut down both sides of the monkfish tail using a sharp knife. Remove the bone and discard. Cut away and discard any skin if liked, then cut the monkfish into steaks.

In a bowl, combine the sake, lime juice and rind.

Sprinkle both sides of the fish steaks with salt and pepper. Away from the hot coals, lightly brush the grill rack with with oil. Cook the fish for 2–3 minutes on each side, or until it changes colour and flakes easily with a fork. Remove from the grill and brush each with the combined sake, juice and rind.

To serve, arrange the spinach leaves on serving plates and top with the fish steaks. Serve with extra lime rind.

Monkfish with Vegetables

Serves 4

300 g/10 oz parsnips, peeled
350 g/12 oz sweet potatoes, peeled
300 g/10 oz carrots, peeled
2 onions, peeled
4–6 garlic cloves, peeled
salt and freshly ground
black pepper
2 tbsp olive oil
2 small monkfish tails,
about 900 g/2 lb total weight, or
4 monkfish fillets,
about 700 g/1½ lb total weight
2–3 sprigs of fresh rosemary
2 yellow peppers, deseeded
225 g/8 oz cherry tomatoes

Prepare a covered barbecue, or preheat the oven to 190°C/375°F/ Gas Mark 5. Cut all the root vegetables, including the onions, into even-sized wedges and place in a large barbecue tray or roasting tin. Reserve 2 garlic cloves and add the remainder to the roasting tin. Season to taste with salt and pepper and pour over 1 tablespoon of the oil. Turn the vegetables over until lightly coated in the oil, then cook in the barbecue or oven for 20 minutes.

Meanwhile, cut the monkfish tails into fillets. Using a sharp knife, cut down both sides of the central bone to form 2 fillets from each tail. Discard any skin or membrane, then rinse thoroughly. Make small incisions down the length of the monkfish fillets.

Cut the reserved garlic cloves into small slivers and break the rosemary into small sprigs. Insert the garlic and rosemary into the incisions in the fish.

Cut the peppers into strips, then add to the tray together with the cherry tomatoes. Place the fish on top and drizzle with the remaining oil. Cook for a further 12–15 minutes, or until the vegetables and fish are thoroughly cooked. Serve.

Meat & Poultry

There is a whole world of meat and poultry out there to cook on the barbecue, and as many styles and flavours to impart. Conjure up a little of the Caribbean with some Jamaican Jerk Pork or go Middle Eastern with Spicy Chicken Skewers with Mango Tabbouleh; please kids and adults alike with Cheesy Chicken Burgers or elevate your evening with Spatchcocked Poussins with Garlic Sage Butter. Whatever you choose, you'll be sure to enjoy some deliciously succulent and artfully grilled delights.

Jamaican Jerk Pork

Serves 4

2 onions, peeled and chopped
2 garlic cloves, peeled and crushed
4 tbsp lime juice
2 tbsp each dark molasses, soy sauce
and chopped fresh root ginger
2 jalapeño chillies, deseeded and
chopped
½ tsp ground cinnamon
¼ tsp each ground allspice,
ground nutmeg
4 pork loin chops, on the bone

For the rice

175 g/6 oz dried red kidney beans,
soaked overnight
1 tbsp vegetable oil
1 onion, peeled and finely chopped
1 celery stalk, trimmed and finely sliced
3 garlic cloves, peeled and crushed
2 bay leaves
225 g/8 oz long-grain white rice
475 ml/18 fl oz chicken or ham stock
sprigs of fresh flat-leaf parsley, to garnish

To make the jerk pork marinade, purée the onions, garlic, lime juice, molasses, soy sauce, ginger, chillies, cinnamon, allspice and nutmeg together in a food processor until smooth. Put the pork chops into a plastic or non-reactive dish and pour over the marinade, turning the chops to coat. Marinate in the refrigerator for at least 1 hour or overnight.

For the rice, drain the beans and place in a large saucepan with about 2 litres/3½ pints cold water. Bring to the boil and boil rapidly for 10 minutes. Reduce the heat, cover and simmer gently, for 1 hour until tender, adding more water if necessary. When cooked, drain well and mash roughly. Heat the oil for the rice in a saucepan with a tight-fitting lid and add the onion, celery and garlic. Cook gently for 5 minutes until softened. Add the bay leaves, rice and stock and stir. Bring to the boil, cover and cook very gently for 10 minutes. Add the beans and stir well again. Cook for a further 5 minutes, then remove from the heat. Meanwhile, prepare the barbecue.

When the barbecue is ready, or you have heated a griddle pan until almost smoking, remove the pork chops from the marinade, scraping off any surplus and add to the barbecue or pan. Cook for 5–8 minutes on each side, or until cooked. Garnish with the parsley and serve immediately with the rice, if using, or fresh salad.

Jerked Steaks

Serves 4–6

4 rump/sirloin steaks, 125 g/4 oz each

For the jerk sauce
1 tsp ground allspice
25 g/1 oz light muscovado sugar
1–2 garlic cloves, peeled and chopped
1 small red chilli, deseeded and chopped
few fresh thyme sprigs, leaves removed
1 tsp ground cinnamon
¼ tsp freshly grated nutmeg
salt and freshly ground black pepper
1 tbsp soy sauce

For the mango relish
1 ripe mango, peeled, stoned and
finely chopped
6 spring onions, trimmed and chopped
1–2 garlic cloves, peeled and crushed
1 red chilli, deseeded and chopped
1 small, ripe but firm banana,
peeled and chopped
1 tbsp lime juice
1 tbsp clear honey, warmed
50 g/2 oz unsweetened chopped dates
1 tsp ground cinnamon
salad, potato wedges, to serve (optional)

Blend all the ingredients for the jerk sauce then rub over the steaks. Place on a plate, lightly cover and leave in the refrigerator for at least 30 minutes.

Mix together all the ingredients for the mango relish, cover and leave for 30 minutes to allow the flavours to develop.

Meanwhile, prepare the barbecue or, when ready to cook, heat a griddle pan or heavy-based frying pan until hot and a few drops of water sizzle when dropped into the pan. Add the steaks to the barbecue or pan and cook for 2–3 minutes on each side for rare, 3–4 minutes on each side for medium and 5–6 minutes on each side for well done.

Remove from the barbecue or pan and serve with the prepared relish, salad and potato wedges, if using.

Marinated Lamb Chops

Serves 4

4 thick lamb chops

mixed salad or freshly cooked
vegetables, to serve

For the marinade

1 small bunch of fresh thyme, leaves
removed

1 tbsp freshly chopped rosemary

1 tsp salt

2 garlic cloves, peeled
and crushed

rind and juice of 1 lemon

2 tbsp olive oil

For the garlic-fried potatoes

3 tbsp olive oil

550 g/1¼ lb potatoes, peeled and
cut into 1 cm/½ inch dice

6 unpeeled garlic cloves

Trim the chops of any excess fat, wipe with a clean damp cloth and reserve. To make the marinade, using a pestle and mortar, pound the thyme leaves and rosemary with the salt until pulpy. Add the garlic and continue pounding until crushed. Stir in the lemon rind and juice and the olive oil.

Pour the marinade over the lamb chops, turning them until they are well coated. Cover lightly and leave to marinate in the refrigerator for about 1 hour. Meanwhile, prepare the barbecue.

To make the potatoes, heat the oil in a large barbecue tray or non-stick frying pan. Add the potatoes and garlic and cook over a low heat for about 20 minutes, stirring occasionally. Increase the heat and cook for a further 10–15 minutes until golden. Drain on absorbent kitchen paper and add salt to taste. Keep warm.

Add the lamb chops to the barbecue or a hot griddle pan and cook for 3–4 minutes on each side until golden, but still pink in the middle. Serve with the potatoes and either a mixed salad or freshly cooked vegetables.

Grilled Steaks and Tomatoes

Serves 4

For the saffron potatoes (optional)

700 g/1½ lb new potatoes, halved
few strands of saffron
300 ml/½ pint vegetable or beef stock
1 small onion, peeled and finely chopped
25 g/1 oz butter
salt and freshly ground black pepper

For the tomatoes

2 tsp balsamic vinegar
2 tbsp olive oil
1 tsp caster sugar
salt and freshly ground black pepper
8 plum tomatoes, halved
50 g/2 oz butter (if using a pan)
4 boneless sirloin steaks, each
weighing 225 g/8 oz
2 tbsp freshly chopped parsley

Prepare the barbecue. If making the saffron potatoes, cook the potatoes in boiling salted water for 8 minutes and drain well. Return the potatoes to the saucepan along with the saffron, stock, onion and 25 g/1 oz of the butter. Season to taste with salt and pepper and simmer uncovered for 10 minutes until the potatoes are tender.

Meanwhile, mix together the vinegar, olive oil, sugar and seasoning. Coat the tomatoes in the dressing. Arrange the tomatoes, either cut-side down on the barbecue or cut-side up in a foil-lined grill pan. Grill for 3–6 minutes (if cooking on the barbecue they will take 3–4 minutes if in the centre, or 5–6 minutes if towards the outside), basting occasionally, until tender.

Place the steaks on the barbecue and cook for 4–8 minutes, or to taste and depending on thickness. Or if using a frying pan, melt the butter then add the steaks and cook, again, according to personal preference.

Arrange the potatoes, if using, and tomatoes in the centre of 4 serving plates. Top with the steaks along with any pan juices. Sprinkle over the parsley and serve immediately.

Fillet Steaks with Tomato & Garlic Sauce

Serves 4

700 g/1½ lb ripe tomatoes
2 garlic cloves
2 tbsp olive oil
2 tbsp freshly chopped basil
2 tbsp freshly chopped oregano
2 tbsp red wine
salt and freshly ground black pepper
75 g/3 oz pitted black olives, chopped
4 fillet steaks, about 175 g/6 oz each in weight
salad or freshly cooked vegetables, to serve

Make a small cross on the top of each tomato and place in a large bowl. Cover with boiling water and leave for 2 minutes. Using a slotted spoon, remove the tomatoes and skin carefully. Repeat until all the tomatoes are skinned. Place on a chopping board, cut into quarters, remove the seeds and roughly chop, then reserve.

Peel and chop the garlic. Heat half the olive oil in a saucepan and cook the garlic for 30 seconds. Add the chopped tomatoes with the basil, oregano, red wine and season to taste with salt and pepper. Bring to the boil then reduce the heat, cover and simmer for 15 minutes, stirring occasionally, or until the sauce is reduced and thickened. Stir the olives into the sauce and keep warm while cooking the steaks.

Meanwhile, prepare the barbecue or, when ready to cook, lightly oil a griddle pan or heavy-based frying pan with the remaining olive oil. Cook the steaks for 2 minutes on each side to seal. Continue to cook the steaks for a further 2–4 minutes, depending on personal preference. Serve the steaks immediately with the garlic sauce and salad or freshly cooked vegetables.

Spicy Chicken Skewers with Mango Tabbouleh

Serves 4

8 metal or wood skewers
400 g/14 oz chicken breast fillet
200 ml/7 fl oz natural yoghurt
1 garlic clove, peeled and crushed
1 small red chilli, deseeded and finely chopped
½ tsp ground turmeric
juice and finely grated rind of ½ lemon
sprigs of fresh mint, to garnish

For the mango tabbouleh

175 g/6 oz bulgur wheat
1 tsp olive oil
juice of ½ lemon
½ red onion, finely chopped
1 ripe mango, halved, stoned, peeled and chopped
¼ cucumber, finely diced
2 tbsp freshly chopped parsley
2 tbsp freshly shredded mint
salt and finely ground black pepper

If using wooden skewers, soak them in cold water for at least 30 minutes. Cut the chicken into 5 x 1 cm/2 x ½ inch strips and place in a shallow dish.

Mix together the yoghurt, garlic, chilli, turmeric, lemon rind and juice. Pour over the chicken and toss to coat. Cover and leave to marinate in the refrigerator for up to 8 hours.

Meanwhile, preheat the barbecue, if using. To make the tabbouleh, put the bulgur wheat in a bowl. Pour over enough boiling water to cover. Put a plate over the bowl. Leave to soak for 20 minutes. Whisk together the oil and lemon juice in a bowl. Add the red onion and leave to marinate for 10 minutes. Drain the bulgur wheat and squeeze out any excess moisture in a clean tea towel. Add to the red onion with the mango, cucumber and herbs and season to taste with salt and pepper. Toss together.

Thread the chicken strips on to 8 wooden or metal skewers. Cook on a barbecue or under a hot grill for 8 minutes. Turn and brush with the marinade until the chicken is lightly browned and cooked through. Spoon the tabbouleh on to individual plates. Arrange the chicken skewers on top and garnish with the sprigs of mint. Serve warm or cold.

Cheesy Chicken Burgers

Serves 6

1 tbsp sunflower oil
1 small onion, peeled and finely chopped
1 garlic clove, peeled and crushed
½ red pepper, deseeded
and finely chopped
450 g/1 lb fresh chicken mince
2 tbsp 0%-fat Greek yoghurt
50 g/2 oz fresh brown breadcrumbs
1 tbsp freshly chopped herbs, such as
parsley or tarragon
50 g/2 oz Cheshire cheese, crumbled
salt and freshly ground black pepper

For the sweetcorn and carrot relish

200 g can sweetcorn, drained
1 carrot, peeled, grated
½ green chilli, deseeded and finely chopped
2 tsp cider vinegar
2 tsp light soft brown sugar

To serve

wholemeal or granary rolls
lettuce
sliced tomatoes
mixed salad leaves

Prepare the barbecue or preheat the grill. Heat the oil in a frying pan and gently cook the onion and garlic for 5 minutes. Add the red pepper and cook for 5 minutes. Transfer into a mixing bowl. Add the chicken, yoghurt, breadcrumbs, herbs and cheese and season to taste with salt and pepper. Mix well. Divide the mixture equally into 6 and shape into burgers. Cover and chill in the refrigerator for at least 20 minutes.

To make the relish, put all the ingredients in a small saucepan with 1 tablespoon of water and heat gently, stirring occasionally, until all the sugar has dissolved. Cover and cook over a low heat for 2 minutes, then uncover and cook for a further minute, or until the relish is thick.

Place the burgers carefully directly onto the barbecue (or onto a lightly oiled griddle plate on the barbecue if you are worried about them breaking up), or place under a medium hot grill. Cook for 8–10 minutes on each side, or until browned and completely cooked through. (They will need longer if not directly on the barbecue.) Warm the rolls if liked, then split in half and fill with the burgers, lettuce, sliced tomatoes and the prepared relish. Serve immediately with the salad leaves.

Chilli Beef Burgers

Serves 4

1 small red chilli pepper
450 g/1 lb lean minced beef
1 clove garlic, crushed
1 small onion, grated
2 tbsp freshly chopped coriander
1 tbsp vegetable oil, for brushing
125 g/4 oz rocket
20 Vietnamese mint leaves
20 g/¾ oz loosely packed fresh
coriander leaves
1 tbsp chilli oil
salt and freshly ground black pepper
4 crusty rolls, halved
50 ml/2 fl oz Thai sweet chilli sauce
(optional)

Prepare the barbecue, or line a grill rack with kitchen foil and preheat the grill 2–3 minutes before cooking. Cut the top off the chilli. Slit down the side and discard the seeds and membrane (the skin to which the seeds are attached). Finely chop the chilli.

In a bowl, combine the beef, garlic, chilli, onion and chopped coriander. Using wet hands, mix well. Divide into 4 portions and shape each portion into a patty, flattening it slightly to fit the size of the roll.

Brush both sides of the beef patties with vegetable oil and cook on the barbecue or under the grill for 3–4 minutes per side, until cooked through to the centre.

In a bowl, combine the rocket, mint and coriander. Drizzle with chilli oil and season with salt and pepper. Place the greens on the bottom halves of the rolls. Add the beef patties and drizzle with Thai sweet chilli sauce if desired. Add the tops of the rolls and serve.

Soy Beef Skewers

Serves 3–4

12 bamboo skewers
250 g/9 oz sirloin or rump steak
5 tbsp soy sauce
2 tbsp oyster sauce
1 tsp sugar
2 tbsp mirin
2 tsp sesame oil
1 clove garlic, finely chopped
1 tbsp freshly chopped coriander
2 tbsp vegetable oil

Prepare the barbecue, or line a grill rack with kitchen foil and preheat the grill 2–3 minutes before cooking. Soak the skewers in cold water for 30 minutes, then drain.

Slice the steak into thin long strips, about 2.5 x 10 cm/1 x 4 inches. Thread strips onto skewers and place in a shallow nonmetallic dish.

In a bowl, combine 2 tablespoons of the soy sauce, the oyster sauce, sugar, mirin, sesame oil, garlic and coriander, and mix well.

Brush the marinade over the beef, cover with clingfilm and refrigerate for 30 minutes, then drain off the marinade.

Away from the hot coals, lightly brush the barbecue grill rack with oil. Cook the skewers on the barbecue or under the preheated grill for 2–3 minutes until tender, turning when necessary.

Remove from the grill and serve hot with the remaining soy sauce as a dipping sauce.

Turkey Escalopes with Apricot Chutney

Serves 4

4 x 175–225 g/6–8 oz turkey steaks
1 tbsp plain flour
salt and freshly ground black pepper
1 tbsp olive oil
flat-leaf parsley sprigs, to garnish
orange wedges, to serve

For the apricot chutney

125 g/4 oz no-need-to-soak dried
apricots, chopped
1 red onion, peeled and
finely chopped
1 tsp grated fresh root ginger
2 tbsp caster sugar
finely grated rind of ½ orange
125 ml/4 fl oz fresh orange juice
125 ml/4 fl oz ruby port
1 whole clove

Prepare the barbecue. Put a turkey steak on to a sheet of non-pvc clingfilm or non-stick baking parchment. Cover with a second sheet. Using a rolling pin, gently pound the turkey until the meat is flattened to about 5 mm/¼ inch thick. Repeat to make 4 escalopes.

Mix the flour with the salt and pepper and use to lightly dust the turkey escalopes. Put the turkey escalopes on a board or baking tray and cover with a piece of non-pvc clingfilm or non-stick baking parchment. Chill in the refrigerator until ready to cook.

For the apricot chutney, put the apricots, onion, ginger, sugar, orange rind, orange juice, port and clove into a saucepan. Slowly bring to the boil and simmer, uncovered for 10 minutes, stirring occasionally, until thick and syrupy. Remove the clove and stir in the chopped coriander.

Cook the turkey escalopes, in 2 batches if necessary, on the barbecue or in an oiled and heated griddle pan, for 3–4 minutes on each side until golden brown and tender.

Spoon the chutney on to 4 individual serving plates. Place a turkey escalope on top of each spoonful of chutney. Garnish with sprigs of parsley and serve immediately with orange wedges.

Sticky-glazed Spatchcocked Poussins

Serves 4

4 wooden skewers
2 poussins, each about 700 g/1½ lb
salt and freshly ground black pepper
4 kumquats, thinly sliced (optional)
assorted salad leaves,
crusty bread or new potatoes, to serve

For the glaze

zest of 1 small lemon, finely grated
1 tbsp lemon juice
1 tbsp dry sherry
2 tbsp clear honey
2 tbsp dark soy sauce
2 tbsp wholegrain mustard
1 tsp tomato purée
½ tsp Chinese five-spice powder

Prepare the barbecue or preheat the grill just before cooking, and soak the wooden skewers for 30 minutes. Place one of the poussins breast-side down on a board. Using poultry shears, cut down one side of the backbone. Cut down the other side of the backbone. Remove the bone. Open out the poussin and press down hard on the breast bone with the heel of your hand to break it and to flatten the poussin.

Thread 2 skewers crosswise through the bird to keep it flat, ensuring that each skewer goes through a wing and out through the leg on the opposite side. Repeat with the other bird. Season both sides of the bird with salt and pepper.

To make the glaze, mix together the lemon zest and juice, sherry, honey, soy sauce, mustard, tomato purée and Chinese five-spice powder and use to brush all over the poussins.

Place the poussins skin-side up on the barbecue or skin-side down on a grill rack and cook on a medium heat for 15 minutes, brushing halfway through with more glaze. Turn the poussins over and cook for 10 minutes. Brush again with glaze and cook for a further 15 minutes until well-browned and cooked through. If they start to brown too quickly, move the poussins to the edge of the barbecue or turn the grill down. Remove the skewers and cut each poussin in half along the breastbone. Serve immediately with the kumquat slices, if using, salad, crusty bread or new potatoes. If using a grill, you can grill the kumquats on top of the birds before serving.

Chicken & New Potatoes on Rosemary Skewers

Serves 4

8 thick fresh rosemary stems,
at least 23 cm/9 inches long
3–4 tbsp extra-virgin olive oil
2 garlic cloves, peeled and crushed
1 tsp freshly chopped thyme
grated rind and juice of 1 lemon
salt and freshly ground black pepper
4 skinless chicken breast fillets
16 small new potatoes, peeled or
scrubbed
8 very small onions or shallots, peeled
1 large yellow or red pepper, deseeded
lemon wedges, to garnish
parsley-flavoured cooked rice, to serve

Prepare the barbecue, or preheat the grill and line the grill rack with kitchen foil just before cooking. Strip the leaves from the rosemary stems, leaving about 5 cm/2 inches of soft leaves at the top. Chop the leaves coarsely and reserve. Using a sharp knife, cut the thicker woody ends of the stems to a point which can pierce the chicken pieces and potatoes. Blend the chopped rosemary, oil, garlic, thyme and lemon rind and juice in a shallow dish. Season to taste with salt and pepper. Cut the chicken into 4 cm/½ inch cubes, add to the flavoured oil and stir well. Cover, refrigerate for at least 30 minutes, turning occasionally.

Cook the potatoes in lightly salted boiling water for 10–12 minutes until just tender. Add the onions to the potatoes 2 minutes before the end of the cooking time. Drain, rinse under cold running water and leave to cool. Cut the pepper into 2.5 cm/1 inch squares.

Beginning with a piece of chicken and starting with the pointed end of the skewer, alternately thread equal amounts of chicken, potato, pepper and onion onto each rosemary skewer. Cover the leafy ends of the skewers with kitchen foil to stop them from burning. Do not thread the chicken and vegetables too closely together on the skewer or the chicken may not cook completely. Cook the kebabs for 15 minutes, or until tender and golden, turning and brushing lightly with a little extra marinade. Remove the kitchen foil, garnish with lemon wedges and serve on rice.

Spatchcocked Poussins with Garlic Sage Butter

Serves 4

8 wooden skewers

For the herb butter

6 large garlic cloves
150 g/5 oz butter, softened
2 tbsp freshly snipped chives
2 tbsp freshly chopped sage
juice and grated rind of 1 small lemon
salt and freshly ground black pepper

For the poussins

4 spatchcocked poussins
2 tbsp extra-virgin olive oil

To garnish

chives
fresh sage leaves

To serve

grilled polenta
grilled tomatoes

Prepare the barbecue, or preheat the grill and line the grill rack with foil, just before cooking. Soak the skewers 30 minutes before cooking. Put the garlic cloves in a small saucepan and cover with cold water. Bring to the boil, then simmer for 5 minutes, or until softened. Drain and cool slightly. Cut off the root end of each clove and squeeze the softened garlic into a bowl. Pound the garlic until smooth, then beat in the butter, chives, sage and lemon rind and juice. Season to taste with salt and pepper.

Using your fingertips, gently loosen the skin from each poussin breast by sliding your hand between the skin and the flesh. Push one quarter of the herb butter under the skin, spreading evenly over the breast and the top of the thighs. Pull the neck skin gently to tighten the skin over the breast and tuck under the bird. Repeat with the remaining birds and herb butter.

Thread 2 wooden skewers crossways through each bird, from one wing through the opposite leg, to keep the poussin flat. Repeat with the remaining birds, brush with the olive oil and season with salt and pepper. Arrange the poussins on the barbecue or grill rack and cook for 25 minutes, turning occasionally, until golden and crisp and the juices run clear when a thigh is pierced with a sharp knife or skewer. If they start to brown too quickly, move the poussins to the edge of the barbecue or turn the grill down. Garnish with chives and sage leaves and serve immediately with grilled polenta and a few grilled tomatoes.

Marinated Pheasant Breasts with Grilled Polenta

Serves 4

3 tbsp extra-virgin olive oil
1 tbsp freshly chopped rosemary or
sage leaves
½ tsp ground cinnamon
grated zest of 1 orange
salt and freshly ground black pepper
8 pheasant or wood pigeon breasts
600 ml/1 pint water
125 g/4 oz quick-cook polenta
2 tbsp butter, diced
40 g/1½ oz Parmesan cheese, grated
1–2 tbsp freshly chopped parsley
assorted salad leaves and tomatoes,
to serve

Prepare the barbecue, or preheat the grill just before cooking. Blend 2 tablespoons of the olive oil with the rosemary or sage, cinnamon and orange zest and season to taste with salt and pepper.

Place the pheasant breasts in a large, shallow dish, pour over the oil and marinate until required, turning occasionally.

Bring the water and 1 teaspoon of salt to the boil in a large, heavy-based saucepan. Slowly whisk in the polenta in a thin, steady stream. Reduce the heat and simmer for 5–10 minutes, or until very thick, stirring constantly. Stir the butter and cheese into the polenta, then the parsley and a little black pepper.

Turn the polenta out on to a lightly oiled, non-stick baking tray and spread into an even layer about 2 cm/¾ inch thick. Leave to cool, then chill in the refrigerator for about 1 hour, or until the polenta is chilled. Turn the cold polenta on to a work surface. Cut into 10 cm/ 4 inch squares. Brush with olive oil and arrange on the barbecue or grill rack. Cook for 2–3 minutes on each side until crisp and golden, then cut each square into triangles and keep warm.

Transfer the marinated pheasant breasts to the barbecue or grill rack and cook for at least 5 minutes, or until crisp and beginning to colour, turning once. Serve the pheasants immediately with the polenta triangles, salad leaves and tomatoes.

Mixed Satay Sticks

Serves 4

8 bamboo skewers
12 large raw prawns
350 g/12 oz beef rump steak
1 tbsp lemon juice
1 garlic clove, peeled and crushed
salt
2 tsp soft dark brown sugar
1 tsp ground cumin
1 tsp ground coriander
¼ tsp ground turmeric
1 tbsp groundnut oil
fresh coriander leaves, to garnish

For the spicy peanut sauce

1 shallot, peeled and
very finely chopped
1 tsp demerara sugar
50 g/2 oz creamed coconut, chopped
pinch of chilli powder
1 tbsp dark soy sauce
125 g/4 oz crunchy peanut butter

Prepare the barbecue, or preheat the grill on high just before cooking. Soak the skewers in cold water for at least 30 minutes. Peel the prawns, leaving the tails on. Using a sharp knife, remove the black vein along the back of the prawns. Cut the beef into 1 cm ½ inch wide strips. Place the prawns and beef in separate bowls and sprinkle each with ½ tablespoon of the lemon juice. Mix together the garlic, pinch of salt, sugar, cumin, coriander, turmeric and groundnut oil to make a paste. Lightly brush over the prawns and beef. Cover and place in the refrigerator, to marinate for at least 30 minutes, but for longer if possible.

Meanwhile, make the sauce. Pour 125 ml/4 fl oz of water into a small saucepan, add the shallot and sugar and heat gently until the sugar has dissolved. Stir in the creamed coconut and chilli powder. When melted, remove from the heat and stir in the peanut butter. Leave to cool slightly, then spoon into a serving dish.

Thread 3 prawns each on to 4 skewers and divide the sliced beef between the remaining skewers. Cook the skewers on the barbecue or under the preheated grill for 4–5 minutes, turning occasionally. The prawns should be opaque and pink and the beef browned on the outside, but still pink in the centre. Transfer to warmed individual serving plates, garnish with a few fresh coriander leaves and serve immediately with the warm peanut sauce.

Chicken & Lamb Satay

Serves 4

225 g/8 oz each skinless, boneless
chicken and lean lamb
16 bamboo skewers

For the marinade

1 small onion, peeled and finely chopped
2 garlic cloves, peeled and crushed
2.5 cm/1 inch piece fresh root ginger,
peeled and grated
4 tbsp soy sauce
1 tsp ground coriander
2 tsp dark brown sugar
2 tbsp lime juice
1 tbsp vegetable oil

For the peanut sauce

300 ml/½ pint coconut milk
4 tbsp crunchy peanut butter
1 tbsp Thai fish sauce
1 tsp lime juice
1 tbsp each chilli powder and brown sugar
salt and freshly ground black pepper

To garnish

sprigs of fresh coriander, lime wedges

Cut the chicken and lamb into thin strips, about 7.5 cm/3 inches long and place in 2 shallow dishes. Blend all the marinade ingredients together, then pour half over the chicken and half over the lamb. Stir until lightly coated, then cover with clingfilm and leave to marinate in the refrigerator for at least 2 hours, turning occasionally.

Meanwhile, prepare the barbecue, or preheat the grill just before cooking. Soak the skewers in cold water for 30 minutes before required.

Remove the chicken and lamb from the marinade and thread on to the skewers. Reserve the marinade. Cook on the barbecue or under the preheated grill for 8–10 minutes or until thoroughly cooked, turning and brushing with the marinade.

Meanwhile, make the peanut sauce. Blend the coconut milk with the peanut butter, fish sauce, lime juice, chilli powder and sugar. Pour into a saucepan and cook gently for 5 minutes, stirring occasionally, then season to taste with salt and pepper. Garnish plates with coriander sprigs and lime wedges and serve the satays with the prepared sauce.

Malaysian Beef Satay

Serves 4–6

8 wooden kebab skewers
450 g/1 lb beef steak,
such as rump or sirloin
1 tbsp vegetable oil
1 tsp fennel seeds
1 tsp fenugreek seeds
2 red chillies, deseeded and chopped
2 garlic cloves, peeled and crushed
1 tbsp Thai red curry paste
200 ml/7 fl oz coconut milk

For the satay sauce

1 small red chilli, deseeded and finely
chopped
1 tbsp lime juice
50 ml/2 fl oz fish sauce
2 tbsp smooth peanut butter
1 tbsp roasted peanuts, finely chopped
2 spring onions, trimmed
and finely chopped

Soak the wooden skewers in cold water for 30 minutes. Meanwhile, trim the steak, cut into narrow strips and place in a shallow dish.

Heat the oil in a small frying pan, add the seeds and fry for 30 seconds, or until they pop. Add the chillies, crushed garlic and curry paste and continue to fry, stirring, for 2 minutes. Remove from the heat and gradually blend in the coconut milk and allow to cool. Pour over the beef, cover lightly and leave to marinate in the refrigerator for at least 30 minutes.

Meanwhile prepare the barbecue, or, when ready to cook, preheat the grill to high and line the grill rack with kitchen foil. Drain the skewers and beef, reserving the remaining marinade. Thread the beef strips onto the skewers and place on the barbecue or under the preheated grill for 8–10 minutes, or until cooked to personal preference, brushing occasionally with the remaining marinade.

Meanwhile, place all the ingredients for the sauce in a small saucepan and heat gently for 3–5 minutes, stirring occasionally. Serve with the cooked beef.

Aromatic Duck Burgers
on Potato Pancakes

Serves 4

700 g/1½ lb boneless duck breasts
2 tbsp hoisin sauce
1 garlic clove, peeled
and finely chopped
4 spring onions, trimmed and
finely chopped
2 tbsp Japanese soy sauce
½ tsp Chinese five-spice powder
salt and freshly ground black pepper
freshly chopped coriander, to garnish
extra hoisin sauce, to serve

For the potato pancakes

450 g/1 lb floury potatoes
1 small onion, peeled and grated
1 small egg, beaten
1 heaped tbsp plain flour

Peel off the thick layer of fat from the duck breasts and cut into small pieces. Put the fat in a small dry saucepan and set over a low heat for 10–15 minutes, or until the fat runs clear and the crackling goes crisp; reserve. Cut the duck meat into pieces and blend in a food processor until coarsely chopped. Spoon into a bowl and add the hoisin sauce, garlic, half the spring onions, soy sauce and Chinese five-spice powder. Season to taste with salt and pepper and shape into 4 burgers. Cover and chill in the refrigerator for 1 hour. Prepare the barbecue.

To make the potato pancakes, grate the potatoes into a large bowl, squeeze out the water with your hands, then put on a clean tea towel and twist the ends to squeeze out any remaining water. Return the potato to the bowl, add the onion and egg and mix well. Add the flour, salt and pepper. Stir to blend. Heat about 2 tablespoons of the clear duck fat on a flat griddle pan or frying pan on the barbecue (or on the hob), spoon the potato mixture into 2–4 pattie shapes and cook for 6 minutes, or until golden and crisp, turning once. Keep warm in the oven. Repeat with the remaining mixture, adding duck fat as needed.

Brush the burgers with a little of the duck fat and cook on the barbecue, or under a preheated grill, for 6–8 minutes or longer, turning once. Arrange 1–2 pancakes on a plate and top with a burger. Spoon over some hoisin sauce and garnish with the remaining spring onions and coriander.

Chicken Fillet with Aubergine

Serves 4

4 chicken breast fillets
4 spring onions, coarsely chopped
4 cloves garlic
1 tbsp freshly chopped basil
1 tbsp freshly chopped coriander
85 ml/3 fl oz soy sauce
1 tsp five-spice powder
2 tbsp mirin
1 tbsp fish sauce
1 tsp sesame oil
1 tbsp rice wine
2 tsp sugar
6 aubergines
2 tbsp vegetable oil
50 g/2 oz mizuna leaves, rinsed

Place the chicken in a shallow nonmetallic dish. In a food processor, combine the spring onions, garlic, basil, coriander, soy sauce, five-spice powder, mirin, fish sauce, sesame oil, rice wine and sugar and process for about 30 seconds, until well blended. Pour the marinade over the chicken fillets, cover the dish with clingfilm and refrigerate for 2 hours.

Meanwhile, prepare the barbecue and slice the aubergines lengthwways into 2-mm/¹⁄₁₆-inch slices, cutting each slice in half also if the aubergines were quite large.

Drain the chicken, reserving the marinade. Away from the hot coals, lightly brush the barbecue grill with vegetable oil or heat the oil in a griddle pan. Cook the chicken fillets for 4–5 minutes on each side, until golden and tender, brushing with some of the reserved marinade during cooking. Test the chicken by piercing the thickest part with a skewer; the chicken is cooked if the juices run clear. Remove from the grill or pan.

Lightly brush the aubergine slices with oil and cook on the barbecue or in a griddle pan for 1–2 minutes each side, until golden and tender. Place the remaining marinade into a small saucepan, stir over a medium heat and bring to a boil; allow to boil for 1 minute, then set aside. To serve, arrange the mizuna leaves on serving plates, top with the aubergine slices and then the chicken fillets. Drizzle with warm marinade.

Skewered Chicken

Serves 6

2 chickens, each about 900 g/2 lb
125 ml/4 fl oz lemon juice
1 large onion, grated
2 tsp salt
freshly ground black pepper, or
different flavoured peppers if liked
6 long sturdy wooden, or flat
metal skewers
50 ml/2 fl oz butter, melted
1 tsp paprika
cherry tomatoes, to garnish

Using poultry shears or a very sharp knife, cut each chicken in half lengthwise and remove the backbone. Cut each half into six pieces that are nearly equal in size: halve breast pieces and thighs, chop off the bony end of the leg, and leave the wing intact. Put the chicken pieces in a nonmetallic dish or bowl.

In a bowl, combine the lemon juice, grated onion, salt and pepper(s) to taste. Pour over the chicken pieces, turning them in the marinade to coat. Cover the dish with clingfilm and marinate for 3–4 hours in the refrigerator, turning the chicken occasionally.

Prepare the barbecue, preferably with charcoal, and, if using wooden skewers, soak them in cold water for 30 minutes.

Thread the chicken onto the skewers, placing the thicker pieces in the centre, and packing all the pieces close together. In a small bowl, combine the melted butter with the paprika and brush over the chicken. Cook the chicken on the barbecue, basting frequently with the butter mixture and turning often, for 15–20 minutes or until the chicken is cooked through. Remove the chicken from the skewers if desired and garnish with blistered cherry tomatoes.

To blister cherry tomatoes, cut an 'X' on the bottom of each tomato and thread onto skewers if necessary. Brush with melted butter and cook on the barbecue until the skin blisters and browns lightly.

Barbecue Pork Fillet

Serves 4

2 tbsp clear honey
2 tbsp hoisin sauce
2 tsp tomato purée
2.5 cm/1 inch piece fresh root ginger, peeled and chopped
450 g/1 lb pork tenderloin
salad, to serve (optional)

For the stir-fried veg

3 tbsp vegetable oil
1 garlic clove, peeled and chopped
1 bunch spring onions, trimmed and chopped
1 red pepper, deseeded and cut into chunks
1 yellow pepper, deseeded and cut into chunks
350 g/12 oz cooked long-grain rice
125 g/4 oz frozen peas, thawed
2 tbsp light soy sauce
1 tbsp sesame oil
50 g/2 oz toasted flaked almonds

Prepare a covered barbecue, or preheat the oven to 200°C/400°F/ Gas Mark 6, 15 minutes before cooking. Mix together the honey, hoisin sauce, tomato purée and ginger in a bowl. Trim the pork, discarding any sinew or fat. Place in a shallow dish and spread the marinade over the pork to cover completely. Cover with clingfilm and chill in the refrigerator for 4 hours, turning occasionally.

Remove the pork from the marinade and place it on a large piece of kitchen foil, turning up the sides to envelope it in a parcel, or place it in a roasting tin. Reserve the marinade. Cook on the barbecue with the lid on, or in the preheated oven, for 20–25 minutes, or until the pork is tender and the juices run clear when pierced with a skewer. Baste occasionally during cooking with the reserved marinade. Remove the pork from the barbecue or oven, leave to rest for 5 minutes, then slice thinly and keep warm.

Meanwhile, heat a wok or large frying pan, add the vegetable oil and when hot, add the garlic, spring onions and peppers and stir-fry for 4 minutes or until softened. Add the rice and peas and stir-fry for 2 minutes. Add the soy sauce, sesame oil and flaked almonds and stir-fry for 30 seconds or until heated through. Tip into a warmed serving dish and top with the sliced pork. Serve immediately.

Sweet-&-Sour Spareribs

Serves 4

1.6 kg/3½ lb pork spareribs
4 tbsp clear honey
1 tbsp Worcestershire sauce
1 tsp Chinese five- spice powder
4 tbsp soy sauce
2½ tbsp dry sherry
1 tsp chilli sauce
2 garlic cloves, peeled and chopped
1½ tbsp tomato purée
1 tsp dry mustard powder (optional)
spring onion curls, to garnish

Prepare a covered barbecue, or preheat the oven to 200°C/400°F/ Gas Mark 6, 15 minutes before cooking. If necessary, place the ribs on a chopping board and using a sharp knife, cut the joint in between the ribs, to form single ribs. Place the ribs in a shallow dish in a single layer.

Spoon the honey, the Worcestershire sauce, Chinese five-spice powder with the soy sauce, sherry and chilli sauce into a small saucepan and heat gently, stirring until smooth. Stir in the chopped garlic, the tomato purée and mustard powder, if using.

Pour the honey mixture over the ribs and spoon over until the ribs are coated evenly. Cover with clingfilm and leave to marinate overnight in the refrigerator, occasionally spooning the marinade over the ribs.

When ready to cook, remove the ribs from the marinade and place (wrapped in foil to avoid burning if you prefer) on the coolest part of the barbecue with the lid closed, or in a shallow roasting tin in the oven with a little more marinade spooned over. Reserve the remainder of the marinade. Cook for 35–40 minutes, or until cooked and the outsides are crisp. Baste occasionally with the reserved marinade during cooking. Garnish with a few spring onion curls and serve immediately, either as a starter or as a meat accompaniment.

Thai Chicken Wings

Serves 4

4 tbsp clear honey
1 tbsp chilli sauce
1 garlic clove, peeled and crushed
1 tsp freshly grated root ginger
1 lemongrass stalk, outer leaves
discarded and finely chopped
2 tbsp lime zest
3–4 tbsp freshly squeezed lime juice
1 tbsp light soy sauce
1 tsp ground cumin
1 tsp ground coriander
¼ tsp ground cinnamon
1.4 kg/3 lb chicken wings (about 12
large wings)
6 tbsp mayonnaise
2 tbsp freshly chopped coriander
lemon or lime wedges, to garnish

Prepare a covered barbecue, or preheat the oven to 190°C/375°F/ Gas Mark 5, 10 minutes before cooking. In a small saucepan, mix together the honey, chilli sauce, garlic, ginger, lemongrass, 1 tablespoon of the lime zest and 2 tablespoons of the lime juice with the soy sauce, cumin, coriander and cinnamon. Heat gently until just starting to bubble, then remove from the heat and leave to cool.

Prepare the chicken wings by folding the tips back under the thickest part of the meat to form a triangle. Arrange in a shallow ovenproof dish. Pour over the honey mixture, turning the wings to ensure that they are all well coated. Cover with clingfilm and leave to marinate in the refrigerator for 4 hours or overnight, turning once or twice.

Mix together the mayonnaise with the remaining lime zest and juice and the coriander. Leave to let the flavours develop while the wings are cooking.

Arrange the wings on the barbecue in foil parcels, or on a rack set over a kitchen-foil-lined roasting tin. Cook in a covered barbecue, or roast at the top of the preheated oven, for 50–60 minutes, or until the wings are tender and golden, basting once or twice with the remaining marinade and turning once. Remove from the barbecue or oven. Garnish the wings with lemon or lime wedges and serve immediately with the mayonnaise.

Vegetables

A barbecue does not have to be overflowing with meat. Everyone will appreciate some vegetable-based options to vary choice and to balance the meal and flavours. Veggie alternatives here include Aduki Bean & Rice Burgers and hearty Rice-filled Peppers, while vegetarians and meat-eaters alike will enjoy the Marinated Vegetable Kebabs or Tortellini, Cherry Tomato & Mozzarella Skewers. Add a little extra interest too with the Hot Grilled Chicory & Pears.

Marinated Vegetable Kebabs

Serves 4

8 wooden skewers
2 small courgettes, cut
into 2 cm/¾ inch pieces
½ green pepper, deseeded and cut
into 2.5 cm/1 inch pieces
½ red pepper, deseeded and cut into
2.5 cm/1 inch pieces
½ yellow pepper, deseeded and cut
into 2.5 cm/1 inch pieces
8 baby onions, peeled
8 button mushrooms
8 cherry tomatoes
freshly chopped parsley, to garnish
freshly cooked couscous, to serve

For the marinade

1 tbsp light olive oil
4 tbsp dry sherry
2 tbsp light soy sauce
1 red chilli, deseeded and finely chopped
2 garlic cloves, peeled and crushed
2.5 cm/1 inch piece root ginger,
peeled and finely grated

Soak the skewers in cold water for 30 minutes, then drain. Place the courgettes, peppers and baby onions in a pan of just boiled water. Bring back to the boil and simmer for about 30 seconds. Drain and rinse the cooked vegetables in cold water and dry on absorbent kitchen paper. Thread the cooked vegetables and the mushrooms and tomatoes alternately on to the skewers and place in a large shallow dish.

Make the marinade by whisking all the ingredients together until thoroughly blended. Pour the marinade evenly over the kebabs, then chill in the refrigerator for at least 1 hour. Spoon the marinade over the kebabs occasionally during this time. Meanwhile, prepare the barbecue.

Place the kebabs on a hot barbecue or in a hot griddle pan and cook gently for 10–12 minutes. Turn the kebabs frequently and brush with the marinade when needed. When the vegetables are tender, sprinkle over the chopped parsley and serve immediately with couscous.

Spanish Tomatoes

Serves 4

175 g/6 oz whole-grain rice
600 ml/1 pint vegetable stock
2 tsp sunflower oil
2 shallots, peeled and
finely chopped
1 garlic clove, peeled and crushed
1 green pepper, deseeded and cut
into small dice
1 red chilli, deseeded and
finely chopped
50 g/2 oz button mushrooms,
finely chopped
1 tbsp freshly chopped oregano
salt and freshly ground black pepper
4 large ripe beef tomatoes
1 large egg, beaten
1 tsp caster sugar
basil leaves, to garnish
crusty bread, to serve

Prepare the barbecue (covered if available), or preheat the oven to 180°C/350°F/Gas Mark 4. Place the rice in a saucepan, pour over the vegetable stock and bring to the boil. Simmer for 30 minutes or until the rice is tender. Drain and turn into a mixing bowl.

Add 1 teaspoon of sunflower oil to a small, non-stick pan and gently fry the shallots, garlic, pepper, chilli and mushrooms for 2 minutes. Add to the rice with the chopped oregano. Season with plenty of salt and pepper.

Slice the top off each tomato. Cut and scoop out the flesh, removing the hard core. Pass the tomato flesh through a sieve. Add 1 tablespoon of the juice to the rice mixture. Stir in the beaten egg and mix. Sprinkle a little sugar in the base of each tomato. Pile the rice mixture into the shells.

If using an uncovered barbecue, place the tomatoes in 4 squares of kitchen foil big enough to be folded up into roomy parcels, or if using a covered barbecue or an oven place in a baking dish. Pour a little cold water around the tomatoes, replace their lids and drizzle a few drops of oil over the tops. Close the foil parcels, if using. Cook for about 25 minutes. Garnish with the basil leaves and season with black pepper and serve immediately with crusty bread.

Italian Tomatoes with Curly Endive & Radicchio

Serves 4

1 tsp olive oil
4 beef tomatoes
salt
50 g/2 oz fresh white breadcrumbs
1 tbsp freshly snipped chives
1 tbsp freshly chopped parsley
125 g/4 oz button mushrooms, finely chopped
salt and freshly ground black pepper
25 g/1 oz Parmesan cheese, grated

For the salad

½ curly endive lettuce
½ small piece of radicchio
2 tbsp olive oil
1 tsp balsamic vinegar
salt and freshly ground black pepper

Prepare the barbecue (covered if available), or preheat oven to 190°C/375°F/Gas Mark 5. Lightly oil 4 squares of kitchen foil big enough to be folded up around each tomato into roomy parcels, or a baking tray (for use in the covered barcecue or oven), with the teaspoon of oil. Slice the tops off the tomatoes and remove all the tomato flesh and sieve into a large bowl. Sprinkle a little salt inside the tomato shells and then place them upside down on a plate while the filling is prepared.

Mix the sieved tomato with the breadcrumbs, fresh herbs and mushrooms and season well with salt and pepper. Place the tomato shells on the prepared kitchen foil or baking tray and fill with the tomato and mushroom mixture. Sprinkle the cheese on the top, close the foil parcels, if using, and cook on/in the barbecue or in the preheated oven for 15–20 minutes, until golden brown.

Meanwhile, prepare the salad. Arrange the endive and radicchio on individual serving plates and mix the remaining ingredients together in a small bowl to make the dressing. Season to taste.

When the tomatoes are cooked, allow to rest for 5 minutes, then place on the prepared plates and drizzle over a little dressing. Serve warm.

Stuffed Onions with Pine Nuts

Serves 4

4 medium onions, peeled
2 garlic cloves, peeled and crushed
2 tbsp fresh brown breadcrumbs
2 tbsp white breadcrumbs
25 g/1 oz sultanas
25 g/1 oz pine nuts
50 g/2 oz hard cheese such as Edam
or Cheddar, grated
2 tbsp freshly chopped parsley
1 medium egg, beaten
salt and freshly ground black pepper
salad leaves, to serve

Prepare the barbecue, or preheat the oven to 200°C/400°F/Gas Mark 6. Bring a pan of water to the boil, add the onions and cook gently for about 15 minutes.

Drain well. Allow the onions to cool, then slice each one in half horizontally. Scoop out most of the onion flesh but leave a reasonably firm shell.

Chop up 4 tablespoons of the onion flesh and place in a bowl with the crushed garlic, breadcrumbs, sultanas, pine nuts, grated cheese and parsley.

Mix the breadcrumb mixture together thoroughly. Bind together with as much of the beaten egg as necessary to make a firm filling. Season to taste with salt and pepper.

Pile the mixture back into the onion shells and top with the grated cheese. Place on 4 squares of kitchen foil big enough to fold easily around each, and create 4 parcels for the barbecue, or place on an oiled baking tray for the oven. Cook on the barbecue or in the preheated oven for 20–30 minutes or until golden brown. Serve immediately with the salad leaves. If cooking on a barbecue you may wish to finish them off under the grill to achieve a more crisp top.

Rice-filled Peppers

Serves 4

325 g/11 oz ripe tomatoes
2 tbsp olive oil
1 onion, peeled and chopped
1 garlic clove, peeled and crushed
½ tsp dark muscovado sugar
125 g/4 oz cooked long-grain rice
50 g/2 oz pine nuts, toasted
1 tbsp freshly chopped oregano
salt and freshly ground black pepper
2 large red peppers
2 large yellow peppers

To serve

mixed salad
crusty bread

Prepare the barbecue (covered if available), or preheat the oven to 200°C/400°F/Gas Mark 6. Put the tomatoes in a small bowl and pour over boiling water to cover. Leave for 1 minute, then drain. Plunge the tomatoes into cold water to cool, then peel off the skins. Quarter, remove the seeds and chop.

Heat the olive oil in a frying pan, and cook the onion gently for 10 minutes, until softened. Add the garlic, chopped tomatoes and sugar. Gently cook the tomato mixture for 10 minutes until thickened. Remove from the heat and stir the rice, pine nuts and oregano into the sauce. Season to taste with salt and pepper.

Halve the peppers lengthways, cutting through and leaving the stem on. Remove the seeds and cores, then put the peppers on the barbecue rack or in a lightly oiled roasting tin, cut-side down and cook in the barbecue or the preheated oven for about 10 minutes.

Spoon in the filling to the peppers, then, if using an uncovered barbecue, wrap the tomatoes in foil parcels, or if using a covered barbecue or an oven return to the roasting tin and cover with kitchen foil. Cook for 15 minutes, or until the peppers are very tender, opening the parcels or removing the foil for the last 5 miuntes. Serve one red pepper half and one yellow pepper half per person with a mixed salad and plenty of warmed, crusty bread.

Sweet Potato Cakes with Mango & Tomato Salsa

Serves 4

700 g/1½ lb sweet potatoes, peeled
and cut into large chunks
salt and freshly ground black pepper
25 g/1 oz butter
1 onion, peeled and chopped
1 garlic clove, peeled and crushed
pinch of freshly grated nutmeg
1 medium egg, beaten
50 g/2 oz quick-cook polenta
2 tbsp sunflower oil

For the salsa

1 ripe mango, peeled,
stoned and diced
6 cherry tomatoes, cut in wedges
4 spring onions, trimmed and
thinly sliced
1 red chilli, deseeded and
finely chopped
finely grated rind and juice of ½ lime
2 tbsp freshly chopped mint
1 tsp clear honey
salad leaves, to serve

Prepare the barbecue. Steam or cook the sweet potatoes in lightly salted boiling water for 15–20 minutes, until tender. Drain well, then mash until smooth.

Melt the butter in a saucepan. Add the onion and garlic and cook gently for 10 minutes until soft. Add to the mashed sweet potato and season with the nutmeg, salt and pepper. Stir together until mixed thoroughly. Leave to cool.

Shape the mixture into four oval potato cakes, about 2.5 cm/ 1 inch thick. Dip first in the beaten egg, allowing the excess to fall back into the bowl, then coat in the polenta. Refrigerate for at least 30 minutes.

Meanwhile, mix together all the ingredients for the salsa. Spoon into a serving bowl, cover with clingfilm and leave at room temperature to allow the flavours to develop.

Heat the oil in a flat barbecue tray or a frying pan on the barbecue or on the hob and cook the potato cakes for 4–5 minutes on each side. Serve with the salsa and salad leaves.

Aduki Bean & Rice Burgers

Serves 4

2½ tbsp sunflower oil
1 medium onion, peeled and very
finely chopped
1 garlic clove, peeled and crushed
1 tsp curry paste
225 g/8 oz basmati rice
400 g can aduki beans, drained and rinsed
225 ml/8 fl oz vegetable stock
125 g/4 oz firm tofu, crumbled
1 tsp garam masala
2 tbsp freshly chopped coriander
salt and freshly ground black pepper

For the carrot raita

2 large carrots, peeled and grated
½ cucumber, cut into tiny dice
150 ml/¼ pint Greek yogurt

To serve

wholemeal baps
tomato slices
lettuce leaves

Heat 1 tablespoon of the oil in a saucepan and gently cook the onion for 10 minutes until soft. Add the garlic and curry paste and cook for a few more seconds. Stir in the rice and beans. Pour in the stock, bring to the boil and simmer for 12 minutes, or until all the stock has been absorbed – do not lift the lid for the first 10 minutes of cooking. Reserve.

Lightly mash the tofu. Add to the rice mixture with the garam masala, coriander, salt and pepper. Mix. Divide the mixture into eight and shape into burgers. Chill in the refrigerator for 30 minutes.

Meanwhile, make the raita. Mix together the carrots, cucumber and Greek yogurt. Spoon into a small bowl and chill in the refrigerator until ready to serve.

Heat the remaining oil in a flat barbecue tray or a frying pan on the barbecue or on the hob. Fry the burgers, in batches if necessary, for 4–5 minutes on each side, or until lightly browned. Serve in the baps with tomato slices and lettuce. Accompany with the raita.

Hot Chicory & Pears

Serves 4

50 g/2 oz unblanched almonds,
roughly chopped
4 small heads of chicory
2 tbsp olive oil
1 tbsp walnut oil
2 firm ripe dessert pears
2 tsp lemon juice
1 tsp freshly chopped oregano.
salt and freshly ground black pepper
freshly chopped oregano, to garnish
warmed ciabatta bread, to serve

Prepare the barbecue or preheat the grill to hot. Fry the chopped almonds in a little oil in a pan on the barbecue or cook under a grill on a foil-lined grill pan. Cook for about 3 minutes, moving the almonds around occasionally, until lightly browned. Reserve.

Halve the chicory lengthways and cut out the cores. Mix together the olive and walnut oils. Brush about 2 tablespoons all over the chicory.

Put the chicory on the barbecue in foil parcels, or on a grill pan, and cook on a hot heat for 2–3 minutes, or until beginning to char. Turn and cook for a further 1–2 minutes, then turn again.

Peel, core and thickly slice the pears. Brush with 1 tablespoon of the oils, then place the pears on top of the chicory. Cook for a further 3–4 minutes, or until both the chicory and pears are soft.

Transfer the chicory and pears to 4 warmed serving plates. Whisk together the remaining oil, lemon juice and oregano and season to taste with salt and pepper.

Drizzle the dressing over the chicory and pears and scatter with the toasted almonds. Garnish with fresh oregano and serve with ciabatta bread.

Tortellini, Cherry Tomato & Mozzarella Skewers

Serves 6

8 wooden skewers
250 g/9 oz mixed green and plain cheese
or vegetable-filled fresh tortellini
150 ml/¼ pint extra virgin olive oil
2 garlic cloves, peeled and crushed
pinch dried thyme or basil
salt and freshly ground black pepper
225 g/8 oz cherry tomatoes
450 g/1 lb mozzarella, cut into
2.5 cm/1 inch cubes
basil leaves, to garnish
dressed salad leaves, to serve

Soak the skewers in cold water for at least 30 minutes. Prepare the barbecue, or preheat the grill and line the grill pan with kitchen foil, just before cooking. Bring a large pan of lightly salted water to a rolling boil. Add the tortellini and cook according to the packet instructions, or until *al dente*. Drain, rinse under cold running water, drain again and toss with 2 tablespoons of the olive oil and reserve.

Pour the remaining olive oil into a small bowl. Add the crushed garlic and thyme or basil, then blend well. Season to taste with salt and black pepper and reserve.

To assemble the skewers, thread the tortellini alternately with the cherry tomatoes and cubes of mozzarella. Brush the skewers on all sides with the olive oil mixture then either place on the hot barbecue or place in the grill rack under the preheated grill.

Cook the skewers for about 5 minutes, or until they begin to turn golden, turning them halfway through cooking. Arrange two skewers on each plate and garnish with a few basil leaves. Serve immediately with dressed salad leaves.

Side Dishes
& Salads

No satisfying barbecue party is complete without some side dishes and salads. Take a break from floppy cos lettuce and cucumber, put in a little more thought and your efforts will be rewarded. If fresh and zingy is what you're after, try the Bulghur Wheat Salad with Minty Lemon Dressing or a classic Coleslaw. For something a little more hearty, whip up the Smoked Mackerel & Potato Salad; and for a delicious dip try the Aubergine & Yogurt Dip.

Roasted Aubergine Dip with Pitta Strips

Serves 4

4 pitta breads
2 large aubergines
1 garlic clove, peeled
¼ tsp sesame oil
1 tbsp lemon juice
½ tsp ground cumin
salt and freshly ground black pepper
2 tbsp freshly chopped parsley
fresh salad leaves, to serve

Preheat the oven to 180°C/350°F/Gas Mark 4. On a chopping board cut the pitta breads into strips. Spread the bread in a single layer on to a large baking tray. Cook in the preheated oven for 15 minutes until golden and crisp. Leave to cool on a wire cooling rack.

Trim the aubergines, rinse lightly and reserve. Heat the oil in a griddle pan until almost smoking. Cook the aubergines and garlic for about 15 minutes. Turn the aubergines frequently, until very tender with wrinkled and charred skins. Remove from heat. Leave to cool. (You could grill the aubergines on the barbecue if wished.)

When the aubergines are cool enough to handle, cut in half and scoop out the cooked flesh and place in a food processor. Squeeze the softened garlic flesh from the papery skin and add to the aubergine.

Blend the aubergine and garlic until smooth, then add the sesame oil, lemon juice and cumin and blend again to mix. Season to taste with salt and pepper, stir in the parsley and serve with the pitta strips and mixed salad leaves.

Aubergine & Yogurt Dip

Makes 600 ml/1 pint

2 x 225 g/8 oz aubergines
1 tbsp light olive oil
1 tbsp lemon juice
2 garlic cloves, peeled and crushed
190 g jar pimentos, drained
150 ml/¼ pint natural yogurt
salt and freshly ground black pepper
25 g/1 oz black olives, pitted and chopped
225 g/8 oz cauliflower florets
225 g/8 oz broccoli florets
125 g/4 oz carrots, peeled and cut into
5 cm/2 inch strips

Preheat the oven to 200°C/400°F/Gas Mark 6. Pierce the skin of the aubergines with a fork and place on a baking tray. Cook for 40 minutes or until very soft.

Cool the aubergines, then cut in half, and scoop out the flesh and tip into a bowl. Mash the aubergine with the olive oil, lemon juice and garlic until smooth or blend for a few seconds in a food processor.

Chop the pimentos into small cubes and add to the aubergine mixture. When blended add the yogurt. Stir well and season to taste with salt and pepper. Add the chopped olives and leave in the refrigerator to chill for at least 30 minutes.

Place the cauliflower and broccoli florets and carrot strips into a pan and cover with boiling water. Simmer for 2 minutes, then rinse in cold water. Drain and serve as crudités to accompany the dip.

Sweet Potato Crisps
with Mango Salsa

Serves 6

For the salsa

1 large ripe mango, peeled, stoned
and cut into small cubes
8 cherry tomatoes, quartered
½ cucumber, peeled if preferred and
finely diced
1 red onion, peeled and
finely chopped
pinch of sugar
1 red chilli, deseeded and
finely chopped
2 tbsp rice vinegar
2 tbsp olive oil
grated rind and juice of 1 lime
450 g/1 lb sweet potatoes,
peeled and thinly sliced
vegetable oil, for deep frying
sea salt
2 tbsp freshly chopped mint

To make the salsa, mix the mango with the tomatoes, cucumber and onion. Add the sugar, chilli, vinegar, oil and the lime rind and juice. Mix together thoroughly, cover and leave for 45–50 minutes.

Soak the potatoes in cold water for 40 minutes to remove as much of the excess starch as possible. Drain and dry thoroughly in a clean tea towel, or absorbent kitchen paper.

Heat the oil to 190°C/375°F in a deep fryer. When at the correct temperature, place half the potatoes in the frying basket, then carefully lower the potatoes into the hot oil and cook for 4–5 minutes, or until they are golden brown, shaking the basket every minute so that they do not stick together.

Drain the potato crisps on absorbent kitchen paper, sprinkle with sea salt and place under a preheated moderate grill for a few seconds to dry out. Repeat with the remaining potatoes. Stir the mint into the salsa and serve with the potato crisps.

Stuffed Vine Leaves

Serves 6–8

150 g/5 oz long-grain rice
225 g/8 oz fresh or preserved vine leaves
225 g/8 oz red onion, peeled and finely chopped
3 baby leeks, trimmed and finely sliced
25 g/1 oz freshly chopped parsley
25 g/1 oz freshly chopped mint
25 g/1 oz freshly chopped dill
150 ml/¼ pint extra-virgin olive oil
salt and freshly ground black pepper
50 g/2 oz currants
50 g/2 oz ready-to-eat dried apricots, finely chopped
25 g/1 oz pine nuts
juice of 1 lemon
600–750 ml/1–1¼ pints boiling stock
lemon wedges or slices, to garnish
4 tbsp Greek-style yogurt, to serve

Soak the rice in cold water for 30 minutes. If using fresh vine leaves, blanch 5–6 leaves at a time in salted boiling water for a minute. Rinse and drain. If using preserved vine leaves, soak in tepid water for at least 20 minutes, drain, rinse and pat dry with absorbent kitchen paper.

Mix the onion and leeks with the herbs and half the oil. Add the drained rice, mix and season to taste with salt and pepper. Stir in the currants, apricots, pine nuts and lemon juice. Spoon 1 teaspoon of the filling on to the stalk end of each leaf. Roll, tucking the side flaps into the centre to create a neat parcel; do not roll too tight. Continue until all the filling is used.

Layer half the remaining vine leaves over the base of a large frying pan. Pack the little parcels in the frying pan and cover with the remaining leaves.

Pour in enough stock to just cover the vine leaves, add a pinch of salt and bring to the boil. Reduce the heat, cover and simmer for 45–55 minutes, or until the rice is sticky and tender. Leave to stand for 10 minutes. Drain the stock. Garnish with lemon wedges and serve hot with the Greek yogurt.

Peperonata

Serves 6

2 red peppers
2 yellow peppers
450 g/1 lb waxy potatoes
1 large onion
2 tbsp good quality virgin olive oil
700 g/1½ lb tomatoes, peeled,
deseeded and chopped
2 small courgettes
50 g/2 oz pitted black olives,
quartered
small handful basil leaves
salt and freshly ground black pepper
crusty bread, to serve

Prepare the peppers by halving them lengthwise and removing the stems, seeds, and membranes.

Cut the peppers lengthwise into strips about 1 cm/½ inch wide. Peel the potatoes and cut into rough dice, about 2.5–3 cm/1–1¼ inch across. Cut the onion lengthwise into eight wedges.

Heat the olive oil in a large saucepan over a medium heat. Add the onion and cook for about 5 minutes, or until starting to brown.

Add the peppers, potatoes, tomatoes, courgettes, black olives and about four torn basil leaves. Season to taste with salt and pepper.

Stir the mixture, cover and cook over a very low heat for about 40 minutes, or until the vegetables are tender but still hold their shape. Garnish with the remaining basil.

Transfer to a serving bowl and serve immediately, with chunks of crusty bread.

Coleslaw

Serves 6

175 g/6 oz white cabbage
1 medium red onion, peeled
175 g/6 oz carrot, peeled
175 g/6 oz celeriac, peeled
2 celery stalks, trimmed
75 g/3 oz golden sultanas

For the yogurt & herb dressing

150 ml/¼ pint natural yogurt
1 garlic clove, peeled and crushed
1 tbsp lemon juice
1 tsp clear honey
1 tbsp freshly snipped chives

Remove the hard core from the cabbage with a small knife and shred finely. Slice the onion finely and coarsely grate the carrot. Place the raw vegetables in a large bowl and mix together.

Cut the celeriac into thin strips and simmer in boiling water for about 2 minutes. Drain the celeriac and rinse thoroughly with cold water.

Chop the celery and add to the bowl with the celeriac and sultanas and mix well.

Make the yogurt and herb dressing by briskly whisking the yogurt, garlic, lemon juice, honey and chives together.

Pour the dressing over the top of the salad. Stir the vegetables thoroughly to coat evenly and serve.

Crispy Baked Potatoes with Serrano Ham

Serves 4

4 large baking potatoes
4 tsp crème fraîche
salt and freshly ground black pepper
50 g/2 oz lean serrano ham or
prosciutto, with fat removed
50 g/2 oz cooked baby broad beans
50 g/2 oz cooked carrots, diced
50 g/2 oz cooked peas
50 g/2 oz hard cheese such as Edam
or Cheddar, grated
fresh green salad, to serve

Preheat the oven to 200°C/400°F/Gas Mark 6. Scrub the potatoes dry. Prick with a fork and place on a baking sheet. Cook for 1–1½ hours or until tender when squeezed. Use oven gloves or a kitchen towel to pick up the potatoes as they will be very hot.

Cut the potatoes in half horizontally and scoop out all the flesh into a bowl. Spoon the crème fraîche into the bowl and mix thoroughly with the potatoes. Season to taste with a little salt and pepper.

Cut the ham into strips and carefully stir into the potato mixture with the broad beans, carrots and peas.

Pile the mixture back into the eight potato shells and sprinkle a little grated cheese on the top.

Place under a hot grill and cook until golden and heated through. Serve immediately with a fresh green salad.

Beetroot & Potato Medley

Serves 4

350 g/12 oz raw baby beetroot
½ tsp sunflower oil
225 g/8 oz new potatoes
½ cucumber, peeled
3 tbsp white wine vinegar
150 ml/¼ pint natural yogurt
salt and freshly ground black pepper
fresh salad leaves
1 tbsp freshly snipped chives, to garnish

Preheat the oven to 180°C/350°F/Gas Mark 4. Scrub the beetroot thoroughly and place on a baking tray. Brush the beetroot with a little oil and cook for 1½ hours or until a skewer is easily insertable into the beetroot. Allow to cool a little, then remove the skins.

Cook the potatoes in boiling water for about 10 minutes. Rinse in cold water and drain. Reserve the potatoes until cool. Dice evenly.

Cut the cucumber into cubes and place in a mixing bowl. Chop the beetroot into small cubes and add to the bowl with the reserved potatoes. Gently mix the vegetables together.

Mix together the vinegar and yogurt and season to taste with a little salt and pepper. Pour over the vegetables and combine gently.

Arrange on a bed of salad leaves garnished with the snipped chives and serve.

Rice & Papaya Salad

Serves 4

175 g/6 oz easy-cook basmati rice
1 cinnamon stick, bruised
1 bird's-eye chilli, deseeded
and finely chopped
rind and juice of 2 limes
rind and juice of 2 lemons
1–2 tbsp Thai fish sauce
1 tbsp soft light brown sugar
1 papaya, peeled and seeds removed
1 mango, peeled and stone removed
1 green chilli, deseeded
and finely chopped
2 tbsp freshly chopped coriander
1 tbsp freshly chopped mint
250 g/9 oz cooked chicken
50 g/2 oz roasted peanuts, chopped
strips of pitta bread, to serve

Rinse and drain the rice and pour into a saucepan. Add 450 ml/
¾ pint boiling salted water and the cinnamon stick. Bring to the boil,
reduce the heat to a very low heat, cover and cook without stirring
for 15–18 minutes, or until all the liquid is absorbed. The rice should
be light and fluffy and have steam holes on the surface. Remove
the cinnamon stick and stir in the rind from 1 lime.

To make the dressing, place the bird's-eye chilli, remaining
rind and lime and lemon juice, fish sauce and sugar in a food
processor, mix for a few minutes until blended. Alternatively,
place all these ingredients in a screw-top jar and shake until well
blended. Pour half the dressing over the hot rice and toss until the
rice glistens.

Slice the papaya and mango into thin slices, then place in a
bowl. Add the chopped green chilli, coriander and mint. Place
the chicken on a chopping board, then remove and discard any
skin or sinews. Cut into fine shreds and add to the bowl with the
chopped peanuts.

Add the remaining dressing to the chicken mixture and stir
until all the ingredients are lightly coated. Spoon the rice onto
a platter, pile the chicken mixture on top and serve with warm
strips of pitta bread.

Seared Scallop Salad

Serves 4

at least 4 skewers (optional)
12 king (large) scallops
1 tbsp margarine or butter
2 tbsp orange juice
2 tbsp balsamic vinegar
1 tbsp clear honey
2 ripe pears, washed
125 g/4 oz rocket
125 g/4 oz watercress
50 g/2 oz walnuts
freshly ground black pepper

Clean the scallops, removing the thin black vein from around the white meat and coral. Rinse thoroughly and dry on absorbent kitchen paper. Cut into 2–3 thick slices, depending on the scallop size.

If liked, the scallops could be cooked on the barbecue – thread onto pre-soaked skewers, lightly brush with the margarine or butter and cook on a hot barbecue for 1–2 minutes turning over halfway. Or, heat a griddle pan or heavy-based frying pan, then when hot, add the margarine or butter and allow to melt. Once melted, sear the scallops for 1 minute on each side or until golden. Remove from the pan and reserve.

Briskly whisk together the orange juice, balsamic vinegar and honey to make the dressing and reserve.

With a small, sharp knife carefully cut the pears into quarters, core then cut into chunks. Mix the rocket leaves, watercress, pear chunks and walnuts.

Pile on to serving plates and top with the scallops. Drizzle over the dressing and grind over plenty of black pepper. Serve immediately.

Smoked Mackerel & Potato Salad

Serves 4

½ tsp dry mustard powder
1 large egg yolk
salt and freshly ground black pepper
150 ml/¼ pint sunflower oil
1–2 tbsp lemon juice
450 g/1 lb baby new potatoes
25 g/1 oz butter
350 g/12 oz smoked mackerel fillets
4 celery stalks, trimmed and finely chopped
3 tbsp creamed horseradish
150 ml/¼ pint crème fraîche
1 Little Gem lettuce, rinsed and roughly torn
8 cherry tomatoes, halved

Place the mustard powder and egg yolk in a small bowl with salt and pepper and whisk until blended. Add the oil, drop by drop, into the egg mixture, whisking continuously. When the mayonnaise is thick, add the lemon juice, drop by drop, until a smooth, glossy consistency is formed. Reserve.

Cook the potatoes in boiling salted water until tender, then drain. Cool slightly, then cut into halves or quarters, depending on size. Return to the saucepan and toss in the butter.

Remove the skin from the mackerel fillets and flake into pieces. Add to the potatoes in the saucepan, together with the celery.

Blend 4 tablespoons of the mayonnaise with the horseradish and crème fraîche. Season to taste with salt and pepper, then add to the potato and mackerel mixture and stir lightly.

Arrange the lettuce and tomatoes on four serving plates. Pile the smoked mackerel mixture on top of the lettuce, grind over a little pepper and serve with the remaining mayonnaise.

Wild Rice & Bacon Salad with Smoked Chicken

Serves 4

150 g/5 oz wild rice
50 g/2 oz pecan or walnut halves
1 tbsp vegetable oil
4 slices smoked bacon, diced
3–4 shallots, peeled and finely chopped
75 ml/3 fl oz walnut oil
2–3 tbsp sherry or cider vinegar
2 tbsp freshly chopped dill
salt and freshly ground black pepper
275 g/10 oz smoked chicken or duck breast, thinly sliced
dill sprigs, to garnish

Put the wild rice in a medium saucepan with 600 ml/1 pint water and bring to the boil, stirring once or twice. Reduce the heat, cover and simmer gently for 30–50 minutes, depending on the texture you prefer, chewy or tender. Using a fork, gently fluff into a large bowl and leave to cool slightly.

Meanwhile, toast the nuts in a frying pan over a medium heat for 2 minutes, or until they are fragrant and lightly coloured, stirring and tossing frequently. Cool, then chop coarsely and add to the rice.

Heat the oil in the frying pan over a medium heat. Add the bacon and cook, stirring from time to time, for 3–4 minutes, or until crisp and brown. Remove from the pan and drain on absorbent kitchen paper. Add the shallots to the pan and cook for 4 minutes, or until just softened, stirring from time to time. Stir into the rice and nuts, with the drained bacon pieces.

Whisk the walnut oil, vinegar, half the dill and salt and pepper in a small bowl until combined. Pour the dressing over the rice mixture and toss well to combine. Mix the chicken and the remaining chopped dill into the rice, then spoon into bowls and garnish each serving with a dill sprig. Serve slightly warm, or at room temperature.

Warm Chicken & Potato Salad with Peas & Mint

Serves 4-6

450 g/1 lb new potatoes, peeled or
scrubbed and cut into bite-size pieces
salt and freshly ground black pepper
2 tbsp cider vinegar
175 g/6 oz frozen garden peas, thawed
1 small ripe avocado
4 cooked chicken breasts, about 450 g/1 lb
in weight, skinned and diced
2 tbsp freshly chopped mint
2 heads Little Gem lettuce
fresh mint sprigs, to garnish

For the dressing

2 tbsp raspberry or sherry vinegar
2 tsp Dijon mustard
1 tsp clear honey
50 ml/2 fl oz sunflower oil
50 ml/2 fl oz extra virgin olive oil

Cook the potatoes in lightly salted boiling water for 15 minutes, or until just tender when pierced with the tip of a sharp knife; do not overcook. Rinse under cold running water to cool slightly, then drain and turn into a large bowl. Sprinkle with the cider vinegar and toss gently.

Run the peas under hot water to ensure that they are thawed, pat dry with absorbent kitchen paper and add to the potatoes.

Cut the avocado in half lengthways and remove the stone. Peel and cut the avocado into cubes and add to the potatoes and peas. Add the chicken and stir together lightly.

To make the dressing, place all the ingredients in a screw-top jar, with a little salt and pepper and shake well to mix – add a little more oil if the flavour is too sharp. Pour over the salad and toss gently to coat. Sprinkle in half the mint and stir lightly.

Separate the lettuce leaves and spread onto a large shallow serving plate. Spoon the salad on top and sprinkle with the remaining mint. Garnish with mint sprigs and serve.

Bulghur Wheat Salad with Minty Lemon Dressing

Serves 4

125 g/4 oz bulghur wheat
10 cm/4 inch piece cucumber
2 shallots, peeled
125 g/4 oz baby sweetcorn
3 ripe but firm tomatoes

For the dressing

grated rind of 1 lemon
3 tbsp lemon juice
3 tbsp freshly chopped mint
2 tbsp freshly chopped parsley
1–2 tsp clear honey
2 tbsp sunflower oil
salt and freshly ground black pepper

Place the bulghur wheat in a saucepan and cover with boiling water. Simmer for about 10 minutes, then drain thoroughly and turn into a serving bowl.

Cut the cucumber into small dice, chop the shallots finely and reserve. Steam the sweetcorn over a pan of boiling water for 10 minutes or until tender. Drain and slice into thick chunks.

Cut a cross on the top of each tomato and place in boiling water until their skins start to peel away. Remove the skins and the seeds and cut the tomatoes into small dice.

Make the dressing by briskly whisking all the ingredients in a small bowl until mixed well.

When the bulghur wheat has cooled a little, add all the prepared vegetables and stir in the dressing. Season to taste with salt and pepper and serve.

Chinese Salad with Soy & Ginger Dressing

Serves 4

1 head of Chinese cabbage
200 g can water chestnuts, drained
6 spring onions, trimmed
4 ripe but firm cherry tomatoes
125 g/4 oz mangetout
125 g/4 oz beansprouts
2 tbsp freshly chopped coriander

For the soy & ginger dressing

2 tbsp sunflower oil
4 tbsp light soy sauce
2.5 cm/1 inch piece root ginger, peeled and finely grated
zest and juice of 1 lemon
salt and freshly ground black pepper
crusty white bread, to serve

Rinse and finely shred the Chinese cabbage and place in a serving dish.

Slice the water chestnuts into small slivers and cut the spring onions diagonally into 2.5 cm/1 inch lengths, then split lengthwise into thin strips. Cut the tomatoes in half and then slice each half into three wedges and reserve.

Simmer the mangetout in boiling water for 2 minutes until beginning to soften, drain and cut in half diagonally. Arrange the water chestnuts, spring onions, mangetout, tomatoes and beansprouts on top of the shredded Chinese cabbage. Garnish with the freshly chopped coriander.

Make the dressing by whisking all the ingredients together in a small bowl until mixed thoroughly. Serve with the bread and the salad.

Curly Endive & Seafood Salad

Serves 4

1 head of curly endive lettuce
2 green peppers
12.5 cm/5 inch piece cucumber
125 g/4 oz squid, cleaned and cut into thin rings
225 g/8 oz baby asparagus spears
125 g/4 oz smoked salmon slices, cut into wide strips
175 g/6 oz fresh cooked mussels in their shells

For the lemon dressing

2 tbsp sunflower oil
1 tbsp white wine vinegar
5 tbsp fresh lemon juice
1–2 tsp caster sugar
1 tsp mild wholegrain mustard
salt and freshly ground black pepper

To garnish

slices of lemon
sprigs of fresh coriander

Rinse and tear the endive into small pieces and arrange on a serving platter. Remove the seeds from the peppers and cut the peppers and the cucumber into small dice. Sprinkle over the endive.

Bring a saucepan of water to the boil and add the squid rings. Bring the pan up to the boil again, then switch off the heat and leave it to stand for 5 minutes. Then drain and rinse thoroughly in cold water.

Cook the asparagus in boiling water for 5 minutes or until tender but just crisp. Arrange with the squid, smoked salmon and mussels on top of the salad.

To make the lemon dressing, put all the ingredients into a screw-topped jar or into a small bowl and mix thoroughly until the ingredients are combined.

Spoon 3 tablespoons of the dressing over the salad and serve the remainder in a small jug. Garnish the salad with slices of lemon and sprigs of coriander and serve.

Warm Fruity Rice Salad

Serves 4

175 g/6 oz mixed basmati and wild rice
125 g/4 oz skinless chicken breast
300 ml/½ pint chicken or vegetable stock
125 g/4 oz ready-to-eat dried apricots
125 g/4 oz ready-to-eat dried dates
3 sticks celery

For the dressing

2 tbsp sunflower oil
1 tbsp white wine vinegar
4 tbsp lemon juice
1–2 tsp clear honey, warmed
1 tsp Dijon mustard
freshly ground black pepper

To garnish

6 spring onions
sprigs of fresh coriander

Place the rice in a pan of boiling salted water and cook for 15–20 minutes or until tender. Rinse thoroughly with boiling water and reserve.

Meanwhile wipe the chicken and place in a shallow saucepan with the stock. Bring to the boil, cover and simmer for about 15 minutes or until the chicken is cooked thoroughly and the juices run clear. Leave the chicken in the stock until cool enough to handle, then cut into thin slices.

Chop the apricots and dates into small pieces. Peel any tough membranes from the outside of the celery and chop into dice. Fold the apricots, dates, celery and sliced chicken into the warm rice.

Make the dressing by whisking all the ingredients together in a small bowl until mixed thoroughly. Pour 2–3 tablespoons over the rice and stir in gently and evenly. Serve the remaining dressing separately.

Trim and chop the spring onions. Sprinkle the spring onions over the top of the salad and garnish with the sprigs of coriander. Serve while still warm.

Warm Leek & Tomato Salad

Serves 4

450 g/1 lb trimmed baby leeks
225 g/8 oz ripe, but firm tomatoes
2 shallots, peeled and cut into thin wedges

For the dressing

2 tbsp clear honey
grated rind of 1 lime
4 tbsp lime juice
1 tbsp light olive oil
1 tsp Dijon mustard
salt and freshly ground black pepper

To garnish

freshly chopped tarragon
freshly chopped basil

Trim the leeks so that they are all the same length. Place in a steamer over a pan of boiling water and steam for 8 minutes or until just tender. Drain the leeks thoroughly and arrange in a shallow serving dish.

Make a cross in the top of the tomatoes, place in a bowl and cover them with boiling water until their skins start to peel away. Remove from the bowl and carefully remove the skins.

Cut the tomatoes into four and remove the seeds, then chop into small dice. Spoon over the top of the leeks together with the shallots.

In a small bowl make the dressing by whisking the honey, lime rind, lime juice, olive oil, mustard and salt and pepper. Pour 3 tablespoons of the dressing over the leeks and tomatoes and garnish with the tarragon and basil. Serve while the leeks are still warm, with the remaining dressing served separately.

Mediterranean Feast

Serves 4

1 small iceberg lettuce
225 g/8 oz baby new potatoes, scrubbed
225 g/8 oz French beans
4 medium eggs
1 green pepper
1 medium onion, peeled
200 g can tuna in brine, drained and
flaked into small pieces
50 g/2 oz hard cheese, such as Edam, cut
into small cubes
8 ripe but firm cherry tomatoes, quartered
50 g/2 oz black pitted olives, halved
freshly chopped basil, to garnish

For the lime vinaigrette
3 tbsp light olive oil
2 tbsp white wine vinegar
4 tbsp lime juice
grated rind of 1 lime
1 tsp Dijon mustard
1-2 tsp caster sugar
salt and freshly ground black pepper

Cut the lettuce into four and remove the hard core. Tear into bite-size pieces and arrange on a large serving platter or four individual plates. Cook the potatoes in boiling salted water for 15–20 minutes or until tender, and the French beans for 8 minutes. Drain and rinse in cold water until cool, then cut both the beans and potatoes in half with a sharp knife.

Boil the eggs for 10 minutes, then rinse thoroughly under a cold running tap until cool. Remove the shells under water and cut each egg into four. Remove the seeds from the pepper and cut into thin strips and finely chop the onion.

Arrange the beans, potatoes, eggs, peppers and onion on top of the lettuce. Add the tuna, cheese and tomatoes. Sprinkle over the olives and garnish with the basil.

To make the vinaigrette, place all the ingredients in a screw-topped jar and shake vigorously until everything is mixed thoroughly. Spoon 4 tablespoons over the top of the prepared salad and serve the remainder separately.

Carrot, Celeriac & Sesame Seed Salad

Serves 6

225 g/8 oz celeriac
225 g/8 oz carrots, peeled
50 g/2 oz seedless raisins
2 tbsp sesame seeds
freshly chopped parsley, to garnish

For the lemon & chilli dressing

grated rind of 1 lemon
4 tbsp lemon juice
2 tbsp sunflower oil
2 tbsp clear honey
1 red bird's eye chilli, deseeded and
finely chopped
salt and freshly ground black pepper

Slice the celeriac into thin matchsticks. Place in a small saucepan of boiling salted water and boil for 2 minutes.

Drain and rinse the celeriac in cold water and place in a mixing bowl. Finely grate the carrot. Add the carrot and the raisins to the celeriac in the bowl.

Place the sesame seeds under a hot grill or dry-fry in a frying pan for 1–2 minutes until golden brown, then leave to cool.

Make the dressing by whisking together the lemon rind, lemon juice, oil, honey, chilli and seasoning or by shaking thoroughly in a screw-topped jar.

Pour 2 tablespoons of the dressing over the salad and toss well. Turn into a serving dish and sprinkle over the toasted sesame seeds and chopped parsley. Serve the remaining dressing separately.

Indonesian Salad with Peanut Dressing

Serves 4

225 g/8 oz new potatoes, scrubbed
1 large carrot, peeled and
cut into matchsticks
125 g/4 oz French beans, trimmed
225 g/8 oz tiny cauliflower florets
125 g/4 oz cucumber, cut into matchsticks
75 g/3 oz fresh bean sprouts
3 medium eggs, hard-boiled and
quartered

For the peanut dressing

2 tbsp sesame oil
1 garlic clove, peeled and crushed
1 red chilli, deseeded and finely chopped
150 g/5 oz crunchy peanut butter
6 tbsp hot vegetable stock
2 tsp soft light brown sugar
2 tsp dark soy sauce
1 tbsp lime juice

Cook the potatoes in a saucepan of boiling salted water for 15–20 minutes until tender. Remove with a slotted spoon and thickly slice into a large bowl. Keep the saucepan of water boiling.

Add the carrot, French beans and cauliflower to the water, return to the boil and cook for 2 minutes, or until just tender. Drain and refresh under cold running water, then drain well. Add to the potatoes with the cucumber and bean sprouts.

To make the dressing, gently heat the sesame oil in a small saucepan. Add the garlic and chilli and cook for a few seconds, then remove from the heat. Stir in the peanut butter.

Stir in the stock, a little at a time. Add the remaining ingredients and mix together to make a thick, creamy dressing.

Divide the vegetables between four plates and arrange the eggs on top. Drizzle the dressing over the salad and serve immediately.

Baby Roast Potato Salad

Serves 4

350 g/12 oz small shallots
sea salt and freshly ground black pepper
900 g/2 lb small even-sized new potatoes
2 tbsp olive oil
2 medium courgettes
2 sprigs of fresh rosemary
175 g/6 oz cherry tomatoes
150 ml/¼ pint soured cream
2 tbsp freshly snipped chives
¼ tsp paprika

Preheat the oven to 200°C/400°F/Gas Mark 6. Trim the shallots, but leave the skins on. Put in a saucepan of lightly salted boiling water with the potatoes and cook for 5 minutes, then drain. Separate the shallots and plunge them into cold water for 1 minute.

Put the oil in a baking sheet lined with tinfoil or roasting tin and heat for a few minutes. Peel the skins off the shallots – they should now come away easily. Add to the baking sheet or roasting tin with the potatoes and toss in the oil to coat. Sprinkle with a little sea salt. Roast the potatoes and shallots in the preheated oven for 10 minutes.

Meanwhile, trim the courgettes, halve lengthways and cut into 5 cm/2 inch chunks. Add to the baking sheet or roasting tin, toss to mix and cook for 5 minutes.

Pierce the tomato skins with a sharp knife. Add to the sheet or tin with the rosemary and cook for a further 5 minutes, or until all the vegetables are tender. Remove the rosemary and discard. Grind a little black pepper over the vegetables.

Spoon into a wide serving bowl. Mix together the soured cream and chives and drizzle over the vegetables just before serving.

Mediterranean Rice Salad

Serves 4

250 g/9 oz Camargue red rice
2 sun-dried tomatoes, finely chopped
2 garlic cloves, peeled
and finely chopped
4 tbsp oil from a jar of sun-dried
tomatoes (or olive oil)
2 tsp balsamic vinegar
2 tsp red wine vinegar
salt and freshly ground black pepper
1 red onion, peeled and thinly sliced
1 yellow pepper, quartered
and deseeded
1 red pepper, quartered and deseeded
½ cucumber, peeled and diced
6 ripe plum tomatoes, cut into wedges
1 fennel bulb, halved and thinly sliced
fresh basil leaves, to garnish

Cook the rice in a saucepan of lightly salted boiling water for 35–40 minutes, or until tender. Drain well and reserve.

Whisk the sun-dried tomatoes, garlic, oil and vinegars together in a small bowl or jug. Season to taste with salt and pepper. Put the red onion in a large bowl, pour over the dressing and leave to allow the flavours to develop.

Put the peppers skin-side up on a grill rack and cook under a preheated hot grill for 5–6 minutes, or until blackened and charred. Remove and place in a plastic bag. When cool enough to handle, peel off the skins and slice the peppers.

Add the peppers, cucumber, tomatoes, fennel and rice to the onions. Mix gently together to coat in the dressing. Cover and chill in the refrigerator for 30 minutes to allow the flavours to mingle.

Remove the salad from the refrigerator and leave to stand at room temperature for 20 minutes. Garnish with fresh basil leaves and serve.

Chef's Rice Salad

Serves 4

225 g/8 oz wild rice
½ cucumber
175 g/6 oz cherry tomatoes
6 spring onions, trimmed
5 tbsp extra virgin olive oil
2 tbsp balsamic vinegar
1 tsp Dijon mustard
1 tsp caster sugar
salt and freshly ground black pepper
125 g/4 oz rocket
125 g/4 oz back bacon
125 g/4 oz cooked chicken meat,
finely diced
125 g/4 oz Emmenthal cheese, grated
125 g/4 oz large cooked prawns,
peeled
1 avocado, stoned, peeled and
sliced, to garnish
warm crusty bread, to serve

Put the rice in in a saucepan of water and bring to the boil, stirring once or twice. Reduce the heat, cover and simmer gently for 30–50 minutes, depending on the texture you prefer. Drain well and reserve.

Thinly peel the cucumber, cut in half, then using a teaspoon, remove the seeds. Cut the cucumber into thin slices. Cut the tomatoes in quarters. Cut the spring onions into diagonal slices.

Whisk the olive oil with the vinegar, then whisk in the mustard and sugar. Season to taste with salt and pepper.

In a large bowl, gently toss together the cooled rice with the tomatoes, cucumber, spring onions and the rocket. Pour over the dressing and toss lightly together.

Heat a griddle pan and when hot cook the bacon on both sides for 4–6 minutes, or until crisp. Remove and chop. Arrange the prepared rocket salad on a platter, then arrange the bacon, chicken, cheese and prawns on top. Toss, if wished. Garnish with avocado slices and serve with plenty of warm, crusty bread.

Warm Potato, Pear & Pecan Salad

Serves 4

900 g/2 lb new potatoes, preferably
red-skinned, unpeeled
salt and freshly ground black pepper
1 tsp Dijon mustard
2 tsp white wine vinegar
3 tbsp groundnut oil
1 tbsp hazelnut or walnut oil
2 tsp poppy seeds
2 firm ripe dessert pears
2 tsp lemon juice
175 g/6 oz baby spinach leaves
75 g/3 oz toasted pecan nuts

Scrub the potatoes, then cook in a saucepan of lightly salted boiling water for 15 minutes, or until tender. Drain, cut into halves, or quarters if large, and place in a serving bowl.

In a small bowl or jug, whisk together the mustard and vinegar. Gradually add the oils until the mixture begins to thicken. Stir in the poppy seeds and season to taste with salt and pepper.

Pour about two thirds of the dressing over the hot potatoes and toss gently to coat. Leave until the potatoes have soaked up the dressing and are just warm.

Meanwhile, quarter and core the pears. Cut into thin slices, then sprinkle with the lemon juice to prevent them from going brown. Add to the potatoes with the spinach leaves and toasted pecan nuts. Gently mix together.

Drizzle the remaining dressing over the salad. Serve immediately before the spinach starts to wilt.

Mediterranean Potato Salad

Serves 4

700 g/1½ lb small waxy potatoes
2 red onions, peeled and
roughly chopped
1 yellow pepper, deseeded and
roughly chopped
1 green pepper, deseeded and
roughly chopped
6 tbsp extra virgin olive oil
125 g/4 oz ripe tomatoes, chopped
50 g/2 oz pitted black olives, sliced
125 g/4 oz feta cheese
3 tbsp freshly chopped parsley
2 tbsp white wine vinegar
1 tsp Dijon mustard
1 tsp clear honey
salt and freshly ground black pepper
sprigs of fresh parsley, to garnish

Preheat the oven to 200°C/400°F/Gas Mark 6. Place the potatoes in a large saucepan of salted water, bring to the boil and simmer until just tender. Do not overcook. Drain and plunge into cold water, to stop them from cooking further.

Meanwhile, place the onions in a bowl with the yellow and green peppers, then pour over 2 tablespoons of the olive oil. Stir and spoon onto a large baking tray. Cook in the preheated oven for 25–30 minutes, or until the vegetables are tender and lightly charred in places, stirring occasionally. Remove from the oven and transfer to a large bowl.

Cut the potatoes into bite-size pieces and mix with the roasted onions and peppers. Add the tomatoes and olives to the potatoes. Crumble over the feta cheese and sprinkle with the chopped parsley.

Whisk together the remaining olive oil, vinegar, mustard and honey, then season to taste with salt and pepper. Pour the dressing over the potatoes and toss gently together. Garnish with parsley sprigs and serve immediately.

Mixed Salad with Anchovy Dressing & Ciabatta Croûtons

Serves 4

1 small head endive
1 small head chicory
1 fennel bulb
400 g can artichokes, drained and rinsed
½ cucumber
125 g/4 oz cherry tomatoes
75 g/3 oz black olives

For the anchovy dressing

50 g can anchovy fillets
1 tsp Dijon mustard
1 small garlic clove, peeled and crushed
4 tbsp olive oil
1 tbsp lemon juice
freshly ground black pepper

For the ciabatta croûtons

2 thick slices ciabatta bread
2 tbsp olive oil

Divide the endive and chicory into leaves and reserve some of the larger ones. Arrange the smaller leaves in a wide salad bowl.

Cut the fennel bulb in half from the stalk to the root end, then cut across in fine slices. Quarter the artichokes, then quarter and slice the cucumber and halve the tomatoes. Add to the salad bowl with the olives.

To make the dressing, drain the anchovies and put in a blender with the mustard, garlic, olive oil, lemon juice, 2 tablespoons of hot water and black pepper. Whiz together until smooth and thickened.

To make the croûtons, cut the bread into 1 cm/½ inch cubes. Heat the oil in a frying pan, add the bread cubes and fry for 3 minutes, turning frequently until golden. Remove and drain on absorbent kitchen paper.

Drizzle half the anchovy dressing over the prepared salad and toss to coat. Arrange the reserved endive and chicory leaves around the edge, then drizzle over the remaining dressing. Scatter over the croûtons and serve immediately.

Panzanella

Serves 4

250 g/9 oz day-old Italian-style bread
1 tbsp red wine vinegar
4 tbsp olive oil
1 tsp lemon juice
1 small garlic clove, peeled and
finely chopped
1 red onion, peeled and finely sliced
1 cucumber, peeled if preferred
225 g/8 oz ripe tomatoes, deseeded
150 g/5 oz pitted black olives
about 20 basil leaves, coarsely torn or left
whole if small
sea salt and freshly ground black pepper

Cut the bread into thick slices, leaving the crusts on. Add 1 teaspoon of red wine vinegar to a jug of iced water, put the slices of bread in a bowl and pour over the water. Make sure the bread is covered completely. Leave to soak for 3–4 minutes until just soft.

Remove the soaked bread from the water and squeeze it gently, first with your hands and then in a clean tea towel to remove any excess water. Put the bread on a plate, cover with clingfilm and chill in the refrigerator for about 1 hour.

Meanwhile, whisk together the olive oil, the remaining red wine vinegar and lemon juice in a large serving bowl. Add the garlic and onion and stir to coat well.

Halve the cucumber and remove the seeds. Chop both the cucumber and tomatoes into 1 cm/½ inch dice. Add to the garlic and onions with the olives. Tear the bread into bite-size chunks and add to the bowl with the fresh basil leaves. Toss together to mix and serve immediately, with a grinding of sea salt and black pepper.

Tortellini & Summer Vegetable Salad

Serves 6

350 g/12 oz mixed green and plain cheese-filled fresh tortellini

150 ml/¼ pint extra virgin olive oil

225 g/8 oz fine green beans, trimmed

175 g/6 oz broccoli florets

1 yellow or red pepper, deseeded and thinly sliced

1 red onion, peeled and sliced

175 g jar marinated artichoke hearts, drained and halved

2 tbsp capers

75 g/3 oz dry-cured pitted black olives

3 tbsp raspberry or balsamic vinegar

1 tbsp Dijon mustard

1 tsp soft brown sugar

salt and freshly ground black pepper

2 tbsp freshly chopped basil or flat leaf parsley

2 quartered hard-boiled eggs, to garnish

Bring a large pan of lightly salted water to a rolling boil. Add the tortellini and cook according to the packet instructions, or until *al dente*.

Using a large slotted spoon, transfer the tortellini to a colander to drain. Rinse under cold running water and drain again. Transfer to a large bowl and toss with 2 tablespoons of the olive oil.

Return the pasta water to the boil and drop in the green beans and broccoli florets; blanch them for 2 minutes, or until just beginning to soften. Drain, rinse under cold running water and drain again thoroughly. Add the vegetables to the reserved tortellini. Add the pepper, onion, artichoke hearts, capers and olives to the bowl; stir lightly.

Whisk together the vinegar, mustard and brown sugar in a bowl and season to taste with salt and pepper. Slowly whisk in the remaining olive oil to form a thick, creamy dressing. Pour over the tortellini and vegetables, add the chopped basil or parsley and stir until lightly coated. Transfer to a shallow serving dish or salad bowl. Garnish with the hard-boiled egg quarters and serve.

Chicken & Pasta Salad

Serves 6

450 g/1 lb short pasta
2–3 tbsp extra virgin olive oil
300 g/11 oz cold cooked chicken, cut into
bite-size pieces (preferably roasted)
1 red pepper, deseeded and diced
1 yellow pepper, deseeded and diced
4–5 sun-dried tomatoes, sliced
2 tbsp capers, rinsed and drained
125 g/4 oz pitted Italian black olives
4 spring onions, chopped
225 g/8 oz mozzarella cheese, preferably
buffalo, diced
salt and freshly ground black pepper

For the dressing

50 ml/2 fl oz red or white wine vinegar
1 tbsp mild mustard
1 tsp sugar
75–125 ml/ 3–4 fl oz extra virgin olive oil
125 ml/4 fl oz mayonnaise

Bring a large saucepan of lightly salted water to the boil. Add the pasta and cook for 10 minutes, or until *al dente*. Drain the pasta and rinse under cold running water, then drain again. Place in a large serving bowl and toss with the olive oil.

Add the chicken, diced red and yellow peppers, sliced sun-dried tomatoes, capers, olives, spring onions and mozzarella to the pasta and toss gently until mixed. Season to taste with salt and pepper.

To make the dressing, put the vinegar, mustard and sugar into a small bowl or jug and whisk until well blended and the sugar is dissolved. Season with some pepper, then gradually whisk in the olive oil in a slow, steady stream until a thickened vinaigrette forms.

Put the mayonnaise in a bowl and gradually whisk in the dressing until smooth. Pour over the pasta mixture and mix gently until all the ingredients are coated. Turn into a large, shallow serving bowl and serve at room temperature.

Turkey & Oven-roasted Vegetable Salad

Serves 4

6 tbsp olive oil
3 medium courgettes, trimmed and sliced
2 yellow peppers, deseeded and sliced
125 g/4 oz pine nuts
275 g/10 oz macaroni
350 g/12 oz cooked turkey
280 g jar or can chargrilled artichokes, drained and sliced
225 g/8 oz baby plum tomatoes,quartered
4 tbsp freshly chopped coriander
1 garlic clove, peeled and chopped
3 tbsp balsamic vinegar
salt and freshly ground black pepper

Preheat the oven to 200°C/400°F/Gas Mark 6, 15 minutes before cooking. Line a large roasting tin with tinfoil, pour in half the olive oil and place in the oven for 3 minutes, or until very hot. Remove from the oven, add the courgettes and peppers and stir until evenly coated. Bake for 30–35 minutes, or until slightly charred, turning occasionally.

Add the pine nuts to the tin. Return to the oven and bake for 10 minutes, or until the pine nuts are toasted. Remove from the oven and allow the vegetables to cool completely.

Bring a large pan of lightly salted water to a rolling boil. Add the macaroni and cook according to the packet instructions, or until *al dente*. Drain and refresh under cold running water then drain thoroughly and place in a large salad bowl.

Cut the turkey into bite-size pieces and add to the macaroni. Add the artichokes and tomatoes with the cooled vegetables and pan juices to the pan. Blend together the coriander, garlic, remaining oil, vinegar and seasoning. Pour over the salad, toss lightly and serve.

Hot Duck Pasta Salad

Serves 6

3 boneless and skinless duck breasts

1 tbsp wholegrain mustard

1 tbsp clear honey

salt and freshly ground black pepper

4 medium eggs

450 g/1 lb fusilli

125 g/4 oz French beans, trimmed

1 large carrot, peeled and cut into thin batons

125 g/4 oz sweetcorn kernels, cooked if frozen

75 g/3 oz fresh baby spinach leaves, shredded

For the dressing

8 tbsp French dressing

1 tsp horseradish sauce

4 tbsp crème fraîche

Preheat the oven to 200°C/400°F/Gas Mark 6. Place the duck breasts on a baking tray lined with tinfoil. Mix together the wholegrain mustard and honey, season lightly with salt and pepper then spread over the duck breasts. Roast in the preheated oven for 20–30 minutes, or until tender. Remove from the oven and keep warm.

Meanwhile, place the eggs in a small saucepan, cover with water and bring to the boil. Simmer for 8 minutes, then drain. Bring a large pan of lightly salted water to a rolling boil. Add the beans and pasta, return to the boil and cook according to the packet instructions, or until *al dente*. Drain the pasta and beans and refresh under cold running water.

Place the pasta and beans in a bowl, add the carrot, sweetcorn and spinach leaves and toss lightly. Shell the eggs, cut into wedges and arrange on top of the pasta. Slice the duck breasts then place them on top of the salad. Beat the dressing ingredients together in a bowl until well blended, then drizzle over the salad. Serve immediately.

Pasta & Pepper Salad

Serves 4

4 tbsp olive oil

1 each red, orange and yellow pepper, deseeded and cut into chunks

1 large courgette, trimmed and cut into chunks

1 medium aubergine, trimmed and diced

275 g/10 oz fusilli

4 plum tomatoes, quartered

1 bunch fresh basil leaves, roughly chopped

2 tbsp pesto

2 garlic cloves, peeled and roughly chopped

1 tbsp lemon juice

225 g/8 oz boneless and skinless roasted chicken breast

salt and freshly ground black pepper

125 g/4 oz feta cheese, crumbled

crusty bread, to serve

Preheat the oven to 200°C/400°F/Gas Mark 6. Spoon the olive oil into a roasting tin and heat in the oven for 2 minutes, or until almost smoking. Remove from the oven, add the peppers, courgette and aubergine and stir until coated. Bake for 30 minutes, or until charred, stirring occasionally.

Bring a large pan of lightly salted water to a rolling boil. Add the pasta and cook according to the packet instructions, or until *al dente*. Drain and refresh under cold running water. Drain thoroughly, place in a large salad bowl and reserve.

Remove the cooked vegetables from the oven and allow to cool. Add to the cooled pasta, together with the quartered tomatoes, chopped basil leaves, pesto, garlic and lemon juice. Toss lightly to mix.

Shred the chicken roughly into small pieces and stir into the pasta and vegetable mixture. Season to taste with salt and pepper, then sprinkle the crumbled feta cheese over the pasta and stir gently. Cover the dish and leave to marinate for 30 minutes, stirring occasionally. Serve the salad with fresh crusty bread.

Marinated Mackerel with Tomato & Basil Salad

Serves 3

3 mackerel, filleted
3 beefsteak tomatoes, sliced
50 g/2 oz watercress
2 oranges, peeled and segmented
75 g/3 oz mozzarella cheese, sliced
2 tbsp basil leaves, shredded
sprig of fresh basil, to garnish

For the marinade
juice of 2 lemons
4 tbsp olive oil
4 tbsp basil leaves

For the dressing
1 tbsp lemon juice
1 tsp Dijon mustard
1 tsp caster sugar
salt and freshly ground black pepper
5 tbsp olive oil

Remove as many of the fine pin bones as possible from the mackerel fillets, lightly rinse and pat dry with absorbent kitchen paper and place in a shallow dish.

Blend the marinade ingredients together and pour over the mackerel fillets. Make sure the marinade has covered the fish completely. Cover and leave in a refrigerator for at least 8 hours, but preferably overnight. As the fillets marinate, they will loose their translucency and look as if they are cooked.

Place the tomatoes, watercress, oranges and mozzarella cheese in a large bowl and toss. To make the dressing, whisk the lemon juice with the mustard, sugar and seasoning in a bowl. Pour over half the dressing, toss again and then arrange on a serving platter.

Remove the mackerel from the marinade, cut into bite-size pieces and sprinkle with the shredded basil. Arrange on top of the salad, drizzle over the remaining dressing, scatter with basil leaves and garnish with a basil sprig. Serve.

Fresh Tuna Salad

Serves 4

225 g/8 oz mixed salad leaves
225 g/8 oz baby cherry tomatoes,
halved lengthways
125 g/4 oz rocket leaves, washed
2 tbsp groundnut oil
4 tuna steaks, each cut into 4 pieces,
about 550 g/1¼ lb total weight
50 g/2 oz piece fresh Parmesan cheese

For the dressing
8 tbsp olive oil
grated zest and juice of 2 small lemons
1 tbsp wholegrain mustard
salt and freshly ground black pepper

Wash the salad leaves and place in a large salad bowl with the cherry tomatoes and rocket and reserve.

Heat the wok, then add the oil and heat until almost smoking. Add the tuna, skin-side down, and cook for 4–6 minutes, turning once during cooking, or until cooked and the flesh flakes easily. Remove from the heat and leave to stand in the juices for 2 minutes before removing.

Meanwhile make the dressing, place the olive oil, lemon zest and juices and mustard in a small bowl or screw-topped jar and whisk or shake well until well blended. Season to taste with salt and pepper.

Transfer the tuna to a clean chopping board and flake, then add it to the salad and toss lightly.

Using a swivel blade vegetable peeler, peel the piece of Parmesan cheese into shavings. Divide the salad between four large serving plates, drizzle the dressing over the salad, then scatter with the Parmesan shavings.

Prawn Salad with Toasted Rice

Serves 4

For the dressing

50 ml/2 fl oz rice vinegar
1 red chilli, deseeded and thinly sliced
7.5 cm/3 inch piece lemongrass
stalk, bruised
juice of 1 lime
1–2 tbsp Thai fish sauce
1 tsp sugar, or to taste

For the salad

350 g/12 oz large raw prawns, peeled,
with tails attached, heads removed
cayenne pepper
1 tbsp long-grain white rice
salt and freshly ground black pepper
2 tbsp sunflower oil
1 large head Chinese leaves or
cos lettuce, shredded
½ small cucumber, peeled, deseeded
and thinly sliced
1 small bunch chives, cut into 2.5 cm/
1 inch pieces
small bunch of mint leaves

Place all the ingredients for the dressing in a small bowl and leave to stand to let the flavours blend together.

Using a sharp knife, split each prawn lengthways in half, leaving the tail attached to one half. Remove any black vein and pat the prawns dry with absorbent kitchen paper. Sprinkle the prawns with a little salt and cayenne pepper and then reserve.

Heat a wok over a high heat. Add the rice and stir-fry until browned and fragrant. Turn into a mortar and cool. Crush gently with a pestle until coarse crumbs form. Wipe the wok clean.

Reheat the wok, add the oil and when hot, add the prawns and stir-fry for 2 minutes, or until pink. Transfer to a plate and season to taste with salt and pepper.

Place the Chinese leaves or lettuce into a salad bowl with the cucumber, chives and mint leaves and toss lightly together. Remove the lemongrass stalk and some of the chilli from the dressing and pour all but 2 tablespoons over the salad and toss until lightly coated. Add the prawns and drizzle with the remaining dressing, then sprinkle with the toasted rice and serve.

Thai Prawn & Rice Noodle Salad

Serves 4

75 g/3 oz rice vermicelli
175 g/6 oz mangetout, cut in half crossways
½ cucumber, peeled, deseeded and diced
2–3 spring onions, trimmed and
thinly sliced diagonally
16–20 large cooked tiger prawns, peeled,
with tails left on
2 tbsp chopped unsalted peanuts
or cashews

For the dressing

4 tbsp freshly squeezed lime juice
2–3 tbsp Thai fish sauce
1 tbsp sugar
2.5 cm/1 inch piece fresh root ginger,
peeled and finely chopped
1 red chilli, deseeded and thinly sliced
3–4 tbsp freshly chopped coriander or mint

To garnish

lime wedges
sprigs of fresh mint

Place the vermicelli in a bowl and pour over hot water to cover. Leave to stand for 5 minutes or until softened. Drain, rinse, then drain again and reserve.

Meanwhile, mix all the dressing ingredients in a large bowl until well blended and the sugar has dissolved. Reserve.

Bring a medium saucepan of water to the boil. Add the mangetout, return to the boil and cook for 30–50 seconds. Drain, refresh under cold running water, drain again and reserve.

Stir the cucumber, spring onions and all but 4 of the prawns into the dressing until coated lightly. Add the mangetout and noodles and toss until all the ingredients are mixed evenly.

Spoon the noodle salad on to warmed individual plates. Sprinkle with peanuts or cashews and garnish each dish with a reserved prawn, a lime wedge and a sprig of mint.

Warm Lobster Salad with Hot Thai Dressing

Serves 4

1 orange
50 g/2 oz granulated sugar
2 Cos lettuce hearts, shredded
1 small avocado, peeled and thinly sliced
½ cucumber, peeled, deseeded and
thinly sliced
1 ripe mango, peeled, stoned and
thinly sliced
1 tbsp butter or vegetable oil
meat of 1 large lobster, cut into bite-size pieces
2 tbsp Thai or Italian basil leaves
4 large cooked prawns, peeled, with tails
left on, to garnish

For the dressing

1 tbsp vegetable oil
4–6 spring onions, trimmed and
sliced diagonally into 5 cm/2 inch pieces
2.5 cm/1 inch piece fresh root ginger,
peeled and grated
1 garlic clove, peeled and crushed
grated zest of 1 lime
juice of 2–3 small limes
1–2 tbsp Thai fish sauce
1 tbsp brown sugar
1–2 tsp sweet chilli sauce, or to taste
1 tbsp sesame oil

With a sharp knife, cut the orange rind into thin julienne strips, then cook in boiling water for 2 minutes. Drain the orange strips, then plunge into cold running water, drain and return to the saucepan with the sugar and 1 cm/½ inch water. Simmer until soft, then add 1 tablespoon of cold water to stop cooking. Remove from the heat and reserve.

Arrange the lettuce on four large plates and arrange the avocado, cucumber and mango slices over the lettuce.

Heat a wok or large frying pan, add the butter or oil and when hot, but not sizzling, add the lobster and stir-fry for 1–2 minutes or until heated through. Remove and drain on absorbent kitchen paper.

To make the dressing, heat the vegetable oil in a wok, then add the spring onions, ginger and garlic and stir-fry for 1 minute. Add the lime zest, lime juice, fish sauce, sugar and chilli sauce. Stir until the sugar dissolves. Remove from the heat, add the sesame oil with the orange rind and liquor.

Arrange the lobster meat over the salad and drsizzle with the dressing. Sprinkle with basil leaves, garnish with prawns and serve immediately.

Chicken Satay Salad

Serves 4

4 tbsp crunchy peanut butter
1 tbsp chilli sauce
1 garlic clove, peeled and crushed
2 tbsp cider vinegar
2 tbsp light soy sauce
2 tbsp dark soy sauce
2 tsp soft brown sugar
pinch of salt
2 tsp freshly ground Szechuan
peppercorns
450 g/1 lb dried egg noodles
2 tbsp sesame oil
1 tbsp groundnut oil
450 g/1 lb skinless, boneless chicken
breast fillets, cut into cubes
shredded celery leaves, to garnish
cos lettuce, to serve

Place the peanut butter, chilli sauce, garlic, cider vinegar, soy sauces, sugar, salt and ground peppercorns in a food processor and blend to form a smooth paste. Scrape into a bowl, cover and chill in the refrigerator until required.

Bring a large saucepan of lightly salted water to the boil. Add the noodles and cook for 3–5 minutes. Drain and plunge into cold water. Drain again and toss in the sesame oil. Leave to cool.

Heat the wok until very hot, add the oil and when hot, add the chicken cubes. Stir-fry for 5–6 minutes until the chicken is golden brown and cooked through.

Remove the chicken from the wok using a slotted spoon and add to the noodles, together with the peanut sauce. Mix lightly together, then sprinkle with the shredded celery leaves and either serve immediately or leave until cold, then serve with cos lettuce.

Oriental Noodle & Peanut Salad with Coriander

Serves 4

350 g/12 oz rice vermicelli

1 litre/1¾ pints light vegetable stock

2 tsp sesame oil

2 tbsp light soy sauce

8 spring onions

3 tbsp groundnut oil

2 hot green chillis, deseeded and thinly sliced

25 g/1 oz roughly chopped coriander

2 tbsp freshly chopped mint

125 g/4 oz cucumber, finely chopped

40 g/1½ oz beansprouts

40 g/1½ oz roasted peanuts, roughly chopped

Put the noodles into a large bowl. Bring the stock to the boil and immediately pour over the noodles. Leave to soak for 4 minutes, or according to the packet directions. Drain well, discarding the stock or saving it for another use. Mix together the sesame oil and soy sauce and pour over the hot noodles. Toss well to coat and leave until cold.

Trim and thinly slice four of the spring onions. Heat the wok over a low heat and then add the oil. Add the spring onions and, as soon as they sizzle, remove from the heat and leave to cool. When cold, toss with the noodles.

On a chopping board, cut the remaining spring onions lengthways four to six times, then leave in a bowl of cold water until tassels form. Serve the noodles in individual bowls, each dressed with a little chilli, coriander, mint, cucumber, beansprouts and peanuts. Garnish with the spring onion tassels and serve.

Crispy Noodle Salad

Serves 4

2 tbsp sunflower seeds
2 tbsp pumpkin seeds
50 g/2 oz rice vermicelli or stir-fry noodles
175 g/6 oz unsalted butter
2 tbsp sesame seeds, lightly toasted
125 g/4 oz red cabbage, trimmed and
shredded
1 orange pepper, deseeded and
finely chopped
125 g/4 oz button mushrooms,
wiped and quartered
2 spring onions, trimmed and
finely chopped
salt and freshly ground black pepper
shredded pickled sushi ginger, to garnish

Preheat the oven to 200°C/400°F/Gas Mark 6, then sprinkle the sunflower and pumpkin seeds on a baking sheet. Toast in the oven, stirring occasionally, for 10–15 minutes or until lightly toasted. Remove from the oven and leave to cool.

Crush the rice vermicelli into small pieces (this is easiest in a plastic bag or while the noodles are still in the packet), and reserve. Melt the butter in a small saucepan and leave to cool for a few minutes. Pour the clear yellow liquid carefully into a bowl, leaving behind the white milky solids. Discard the milky solids.

Heat the yellow, clarified butter in a wok and fry the crushed noodles in batches until browned, stirring constantly and gently. Remove the fried noodles as they cook, using a slotted spoon, and drain on absorbent kitchen paper. Transfer the noodles to a bowl and add the toasted seeds.

Mix together the red cabbage, orange pepper, button mushrooms and spring onions in a large bowl and season to taste with salt and pepper. Just before serving, add the noodles and seeds to the salad and mix gently. Garnish with a little sushi ginger and serve.

Cooked Vegetable Salad with Satay Sauce

Serves 4

125 ml/4 fl oz groundnut oil
225 g/8 oz unsalted peanuts
1 onion, peeled and finely chopped
1 garlic clove, peeled and crushed
½ tsp chilli powder
1 tsp ground coriander
½ tsp each ground cumin and sugar
1 tbsp dark soy sauce
2 tbsp fresh lemon juice
2 tbsp light olive oil
salt and freshly ground black pepper
125 g/4 oz French green beans,
trimmed and halved
125 g/4 oz carrots
125 g/4 oz cauliflower florets
125 g/4 oz broccoli florets
125 g/4 oz Chinese leaves or pak choi,
trimmed and shredded
125 g/4 oz beansprouts
1 tbsp sesame oil

To garnish

sprigs of fresh watercress
cucumber, cut into slivers

Heat a wok, add the oil, and when hot, add the peanuts and stir-fry for 3–4 minutes. Drain on absorbent kitchen paper and leave to cool. Blend in a food processor to a fine powder.

Place the onion and garlic, with the spices, sugar, soy sauce, lemon juice and olive oil in a food processor. Season to taste with salt and pepper, then process into a paste. Transfer to a wok and stir-fry for 3–4 minutes.

Stir 600 ml/1 pint hot water into the paste and bring to the boil. Add the ground peanuts and simmer gently for 5–6 minutes or until the mixture thickens. Reserve the satay sauce.

Cook the vegetables in batches in lightly salted boiling water. Cook the French beans, carrots, cauliflower and broccoli for 3–4 minutes, and the Chinese leaves or pak choi and beansprouts for 2 minutes. Drain each batch, drizzle over the sesame oil and arrange on a large warmed serving dish. Garnish with watercress sprigs and cucumber. Serve with the satay sauce.

Summer Desserts
& Drinks

Finally, treat your guests to some refreshing and fruity treats. From a classic Fruit Salad to a cooling Raspberry Sorbet Crush, or a sweet-tooth satisfying Summer Pavlova to a show-stopping Caramelised Oranges in an Iced Bowl, these recipes will help you to really round off the meal. And don't forget to keep everyone hydrated – we've got just a few select suggestions, from a tantalising non-alcoholic Passionate Peach Melba Smoothie to a good old Mojito.

Fruit Salad

Serves 4

125 g/4 oz caster sugar
3 oranges
700 g/1½ lb lychees, peeled and stoned
1 small mango
1 small pineapple
1 papaya
4 pieces stem ginger in syrup
4 tbsp stem ginger syrup
125 g/4 oz Cape gooseberries or physallis
125 g/4 oz strawberries, hulled
½ tsp almond extract

To decorate

lime zest
mint leaves

Place the sugar and 300 ml/½ pint of water in a small pan and heat, gently stirring until the sugar has dissolved. Bring to the boil and simmer for 2 minutes. Once a syrup has formed, remove from the heat and allow to cool.

Using a sharp knife, cut away the skin from the oranges, then slice thickly. Cut each slice in half and place in a serving dish with the syrup and lychees.

Peel the mango, then cut into thick slices around each side of the stone. Discard the stone and cut the slices into bite-size pieces and add to the syrup.

Using a sharp knife again, carefully cut away the skin from the pineapple. Remove the central core using the knife or an apple corer, then cut the pineapple into segments and add to the syrup.

Peel the papaya, then cut in half and remove the seeds. Cut the flesh into chunks, slice the ginger into matchsticks and add with the ginger syrup to the fruit in the syrup.

Prepare the Cape gooseberries, by removing the thin, papery skins and rinsing lightly. Halve the strawberries, add to the fruit with the almond extract and chill for 30 minutes. Scatter with mint leaves and lime zest to decorate and serve.

Orange Freeze

Serves 4

4 large oranges
about 300 ml/½ pint vanilla
ice cream
225 g/8 oz raspberries
75 g/3 oz icing sugar, sifted
redcurrant sprigs, to decorate

Set the freezer to rapid freeze. Using a sharp knife carefully cut the lid off each orange. Scoop out the flesh from the orange, discarding any pips and thick pith. Place the shells and lids in the freezer and chop any remaining orange flesh.

Whisk together the orange juice, orange flesh and vanilla ice cream, until well blended. Cover and freeze, for about 2 hours, occasionally breaking up the ice crystals with a fork or a whisk. Stir the mixture from around the edge of the container into the centre, then level and return to the freezer. Do this 2–3 times then leave until almost frozen solid.

Place a large scoop of the ice cream mixture into the frozen shells. Add another scoop on top, so that there is plenty outside of the orange shell and return to the freezer for 1 hour.

Arrange the lids on top and freeze for a further 2 hours, until the filled orange shell is completely frozen solid.

Meanwhile, using a nylon sieve press the raspberries into a bowl using the back of a wooden spoon and mix together with the icing sugar. Spoon the raspberry coulis on to four serving plates and place an orange at the centre of each. Dust with icing sugar and serve decorated with the redcurrants. Remember to return the freezer to its normal setting.

Tipsy Tropical Fruit

Serves 4

225 g/8 oz can pineapple chunks in natural juice

2 fairly ripe guavas

1 ripe papaya

2 ripe passion fruit

25 g/1 oz unsalted butter

1 tbsp orange juice

50 g/2 oz creamed coconut, chopped

50 g/2 oz soft light brown sugar

2 tbsp malibu liqueur or white rum

sprigs of fresh mint, to decorate

vanilla ice cream, to serve

Drain the pineapple chunks, reserving the juice. Pat the pineapple dry on absorbent kitchen paper. Peel the guavas and cut into wedges. Halve the papaya and scoop out the black seeds. Peel and cut into 2.5 cm/1 inch chunks. Halve the passion fruit and scoop out the seeds into a small bowl.

Heat the butter in a wok, add the pineapple and stir-fry over a high heat for 30 seconds. Turn down the heat and add the guavas and papaya. Drizzle over the orange juice and cook for 2 minutes, stirring occasionally, taking care not to break up the fruit.

Using a slotted spoon, remove the fruit from the wok, leaving any juices behind and transfer to a warmed serving dish. Add the creamed coconut to the wok with the sugar and pineapple juice. Simmer for 2–3 minutes, stirring until the coconut has melted.

Add the malibu or white rum to the wok and heat through, then pour over the fruit. Spoon the passion fruit pulp on top and serve hot with spoonfuls of ice cream decorated with a sprig of mint.

Summer Pavlova

Serves 6-8

4 medium egg whites
225 g/8 oz caster sugar
1 tsp vanilla extract
2 tsp white wine vinegar
1½ tsp cornflour
300 ml/½ pint Greek-set yogurt
2 tbsp honey
225 g/8 oz strawberries, hulled
125 g/4 oz raspberries
125 g/4 oz blueberries
4 kiwis, peeled and sliced
icing sugar, to decorate

Preheat the oven to 150°C/300°F/Gas Mark 2. Line a baking sheet with a sheet of greaseproof or baking parchment paper.

Place the egg whites in a clean grease-free bowl and whisk until very stiff. Whisk in half the sugar, vanilla extract, vinegar and cornflour, continue whisking until stiff. Gradually, whisk in the remaining sugar, a teaspoonful at a time until very stiff and glossy.

Using a large spoon, arrange spoonfuls of the meringue in a circle on the greaseproof paper or baking parchment paper.

Bake in the preheated oven for 1 hour until crisp and dry. Turn the oven off and leave the meringue in the oven to cool completely.

Remove the meringue from the baking sheet and peel away the parchment paper. Mix together the yogurt and honey. Place the pavlova on a serving plate and spoon the yogurt into the centre.

Scatter over the strawberries, raspberries, blueberries and kiwis. Dust with the icing sugar and serve.

Summer Pudding

Serves 4

450 g/1 lb redcurrants
125 g/4 oz caster sugar
350 g/12 oz strawberries, hulled and
halved
125 g/4 oz raspberries
2 tbsp Grand Marnier or Cointreau
8–10 medium slices white bread,
crusts removed
mint sprigs, to decorate
Greek-set yogurt or fromage frais,
to serve

Place the redcurrants, sugar and 1 tablespoon of water in a large saucepan. Heat gently until the sugar has just dissolved and the juices have just begun to run.

Remove the saucepan from the heat and stir in the strawberries, raspberries and the Grand Marnier or Cointreau.

Line the base and sides of a 1.1 litre/2 pint pudding basin with two thirds of the bread, making sure that the slices overlap each other slightly.

Spoon the fruit with their juices into the bread-lined pudding basin, then top with the remaining bread slices.

Place a small plate on top of the pudding inside the pudding basin. Ensure the plate fits tightly, then weigh down with a clean can or some weights and chill in the refrigerator overnight.

When ready to serve, remove the weights and plate. Carefully loosen round the sides of the basin with a round-bladed knife. Invert the pudding on to a serving plate, decorate with the mint sprigs and serve with the yogurt or fromage frais.

Caramelised Oranges in an Iced Bowl

Serves 4

For the iced bowl
about 36 ice cubes
fresh flowers and fruits

8 medium-sized oranges
225 g/8 oz caster sugar
4 tbsp Grand Marnier or Cointreau

Set freezer to rapid freeze. Place a few ice cubes in the base of a 1.7 litre/3 pint freezable glass bowl. Place a 900 ml/1½ pint glass bowl on top of the ice cubes. Arrange the flower heads and fruits in between the two bowls, wedging in position with the ice cubes. Weigh down the smaller bowl with some heavy weights, then carefully pour cold water between the two bowls making sure that the flowers and the fruit are covered. Freeze for at least 6 hours or until the ice is frozen solid.

When ready to use, remove the weights and using a hot damp cloth rub the inside of the smaller bowl with the cloth until it loosens sufficiently for you to remove the bowl. Place the larger bowl in the sink or washing-up bowl, half filled with very hot water. Leave for about 30 seconds or just long enough for the ice to loosen. Remove the bowl and leave in the refrigerator. Return the freezer to its normal setting.

Thinly pare the rind from two oranges and then cut into julienne strips. Using a sharp knife cut away the rind and pith from all the oranges, holding over a bowl to catch the juices. Slice the oranges, discarding any pips and reform each orange back to its original shape. Secure with cocktail sticks, then place in a bowl.

Heat 300 ml/½ pint water, orange rind and sugar together in a pan. Stir the sugar until dissolved. Bring to the boil. Boil for 15 minutes, until it is a caramel colour. Remove pan from heat. Stir in the liqueur, pour over the oranges. Allow to cool. Chill for 3 hours, turning the oranges occasionally. Spoon into the ice bowl and serve.

Raspberry Sorbet Crush

Serves 4

25 g/8 oz raspberries, thawed if frozen
grated rind and juice of 1 lime
300 ml/½ pint orange juice
225 g/8 oz caster sugar
2 medium egg whites

Set the freezer to rapid freeze. If using fresh raspberries pick over and lightly rinse. Place the raspberries in a dish and, using a masher, mash to a chunky purée.

Place the lime rind and juice, orange juice and half the caster sugar in a large heavy-based saucepan. Heat gently, stirring frequently, until the sugar is dissolved. Bring to the boil and boil rapidly for about 5 minutes.

Remove the pan from the heat and pour carefully into a freezable container. Leave to cool, then place in the freezer and freeze for 2 hours, stirring occasionally to break up the ice crystals.

Fold the ice mixture into the raspberry purée with a metal spoon and freeze for a further 2 hours, stirring occasionally.

Whisk the egg whites until stiff. Then gradually whisk in the remaining caster sugar a tablespoon at a time until the egg white mixture is stiff and glossy.

Fold into the raspberry sorbet with a metal spoon and freeze for 1 hour. Spoon into tall glasses and serve immediately. Remember to return the freezer to its normal setting.

Coconut Sorbet with Mango Sauce

Serves 4

2 sheets gelatine
250 g/9 oz caster sugar
600 ml/1 pint coconut milk
2 ripe mangos, peeled, pitted and sliced
2 tbsp icing sugar
zest and juice of 1 lime

Set the freezer to rapid freeze, 2 hours before freezing the sorbet. Place the sheets of gelatine in a shallow dish, pour over cold water to cover and leave for 15 minutes. Squeeze out excess moisture before use.

Meanwhile, place the caster sugar and 300 ml/½ pint of the coconut milk in a heavy-based saucepan and heat gently, stirring occasionally, until the sugar has dissolved. Remove from the heat.

Add the soaked gelatine to the saucepan and stir gently until dissolved. Stir in the remaining coconut milk. Leave until cold.

Pour the gelatine and coconut mixture into a freezable container and place in the freezer. Leave for at least 1 hour, or until the mixture has started to form ice crystals. Remove and beat with a spoon, then return to the freezer and continue to freeze until the mixture is frozen, beating at least twice more during this time.

Meanwhile, make the sauce. Place the sliced mango, icing sugar and the lime zest and juice in a food processor and blend until smooth. Spoon into a small jug.

Leave the sorbet to soften in the refrigerator for at least 30 minutes before serving. Serve scoops of sorbet on individual plates with a little of the mango sauce poured over. Remember to turn the freezer to normal setting.

Stir-fried Bananas & Peaches with Rum Butterscotch Sauce

Serves 4

2 medium-firm bananas
1 tbsp caster sugar
2 tsp lime juice
4 firm, ripe peaches or nectarines
1 tbsp sunflower oil

For the rum butterscotch sauce

50 g/2 oz unsalted butter
50 g/2 oz soft light brown sugar
125 g/4 oz demerara sugar
300 ml/½ pint double cream
2 tbsp dark rum

Peel the bananas and cut into 2.5 cm/1 inch diagonal slices. Place in a bowl and sprinkle with the caster sugar and lime juice and stir until lightly coated. Reserve.

Place the peaches or nectarines in a large bowl and pour over boiling water to cover. Leave for 30 seconds, then plunge them into cold water and peel off their skins. Cut each one into 8 thick slices, discarding the stone.

Heat a wok, add the oil and swirl it round the wok to coat the sides. Add the fruit and cook for 3–4 minutes, shaking the wok and gently turning the fruit until lightly browned. Spoon the fruit into a warmed serving bowl and clean the wok with absorbent kitchen paper.

Add the butter and sugars to the wok and stir continuously over a very low heat until the sugar has dissolved. Remove from the heat and leave to cool for 2–3 minutes.

Stir the cream and rum into the sugar syrup and return to the heat. Bring to the boil and simmer for 2 minutes, stirring continuously until smooth. Leave for 2–3 minutes to cool slightly, then serve warm with the stir-fried peaches and bananas.

Stuffed Amaretti Peaches

Serves 4

ripe peaches
grated zest and juice of 1 lemon
75 g/3 oz Amaretti biscuits
50 g/2 oz chopped blanched
almonds, toasted
50 g/2 oz pine nuts, toasted
40 g/1½ oz light muscovado sugar
50 g/2 oz butter
1 medium egg yolk
2 tsp clear honey
crème fraîche or Greek yogurt,
to serve

Prepare the barbecue (covered if available), or preheat the oven to 180°C/350°F/Gas Mark 4. Halve the peaches and remove the stones. Take a very thin slice from the bottom of each peach half so that it will sit flat. Dip the peach halves in lemon juice and arrange on 4 squares of kitchen foil big enough to fold into parcels round each peach, or in a baking tray (to be used in the barbecue or oven).

Crush the Amaretti biscuits lightly and put into a large bowl. Add the almonds, pine nuts, sugar, lemon zest and butter. Work with the fingertips until the mixture resembles coarse breadcrumbs. Add the egg yolk and mix well until the mixture is just binding.

Divide the Amaretti and nut mixture between the peach halves, pressing down lightly. Fold up the foil, if using, and cook on the barbecue, or in the covered barbecue or preheated oven for 15 minutes, or until the peaches are tender and the filling is golden. Remove from the barbecue or oven and drizzle with the honey.

Place two peach halves on each serving plate and spoon over a little crème fraîche or Greek yogurt, then serve.

Passionate Peach Melba Smoothie

Serves 2

1 ripe passion fruit
3 tbsp mango or orange juice
3–4 ripe peaches, stoned
175 g/6 oz fresh or thawed frozen
raspberries
4 scoops vanilla ice cream
4 peach wedges, to decorate
fan wafer biscuits, to serve

Like the dessert of the same name, this smoothie is quick and easy to make and tastes even better than it looks. As with all smoothies, it is important to ensure that the fruit you use is in peak condition.

Reserve 4 raspberries for decoration. Cut the passion fruit in half and scoop out the flesh and seeds. Sieve the flesh if a smoother texture is preferred.

Place the passion fruit in a smoothie machine or blender and add the mango or orange juice, peaches, remaining raspberries and two scoops of ice cream.

If using a smoothie machine, blend on mix for 15 seconds and then on smooth for 45 seconds. In a blender, blend for 1–2 minutes or until smooth.

Pour into glasses and add a scoop of ice cream to each, with a couple of raspberries and wedge of peach. Top with a wafer and serve.

As an alternative, make the smoothie as above, omitting the raspberries but adding more peaches and a little more ice cream. Top with the ice cream, drizzle with raspberry coulis and serve immediately.

Caribbean Slush

Non-Alcoholic

Serves 2

2 ripe papayas
1 ripe mango
300 ml/½ pint chilled pineapple juice
small piece root ginger
4 ice cubes
2 pineapple wedges, to decorate

Enjoy this cooling drink when the heat is up and you are relaxing round a pool, in the garden or just need a cool down.

Peel the papaya, discard the seeds and cut the flesh into chunks.

Peel the mango and cut the flesh away from the stone, chop the flesh and place in a smoothie machine or blender with the papaya flesh and pineapple juice.

Peel the ginger, grate and add to the machine with the ice cubes.

If using a smoothie machine, blend on mix for 15 seconds and then on smooth for 45 seconds. In a blender, blend for 1–2 minutes or until a 'slush' is formed.

Pour into chilled glasses, decorate with the pineapple wedges and serve immediately.

As an alternative, replace the root ginger with a little finely grated lime rind and two tablespoons of lime juice.

Sea Breeze

Serves 2

1 measure vodka
2–3 measures (or to taste)
cranberry juice
1–2 measures (or to taste)
grapefruit juice
4 ice cubes
orange slice and fresh cranberries if
available, to garnish

Back in the 1930s this cocktail was made with gin, grenadine and lemon juice. However, over the years it has developed into this very popular, and has to be said, delicious cocktail.

Place the vodka in a cocktail shaker and add the cranberry and grapefruit juice to taste. Shake until blended.

Place the ice into a tumbler, pour the cocktail over and serve garnished with an orange slice and a stirrer.

As an alternative, replace the grapefruit juice with pineapple juice to make a Bay Breeze.

Caipirinha

Alcoholic

Serves 2

1 lime
1½–2 tsp caster sugar
4 ice cubes, broken
2 measures cachaça

Caipirinha is the national cocktail of Brazil and is normally made with the country's favourite brandy, cachaça, which is made from sugar cane. The name means 'peasant's drink'. It is made directly in the glass, never in a cocktail shaker.

Cut the lime into small wedges and place with the sugar into an old-fashioned glass (a stubby glass with a thick base, cut glass or clear, that holds about 23 cl/8 fl oz).

Using a spoon crush the lime wedges and sugar together until the juice flows out of the lime.

Add sufficient broken ice to fill the glass then top up with the cachaça and serve.

As an alternative, try passion fruits, kiwi, pineapple, summer berries or grapes in place of the lime. Sometimes soy or dairy milk is added giving a creamy cocktail. Another alternative can be made by using vodka.

Mojito

Alcoholic

Serves 1

4 ice cubes, crushed
2–3 mint sprigs
2 measures white rum
3 tbsp freshly squeezed lime juice
2 tsp (or to taste) demerara sugar
soda water
fresh mint sprig to garnish

One of the most popular summer cocktails around today. This Cuban drink has become the 'wow' both in London and New York regardless of the weather. There are many variations and part of the fun is experimenting with the ingredients to discover which ones best suit your taste buds.

Place half the crushed ice into a glass and add the mint sprigs. Carefully crush the mint on the ice.

Pour the rum, lime juice, sugar and remaining ice into a cocktail shaker and shake until a frost forms on the outside.

Pour the shaker's contents into the glass, top up with soda water, garnish with a fresh mint sprig and serve with a stirrer.

As an alternative, try using other rums such as dark rum or even fruit-flavoured rums, such as mango.

Index

Index